THE
HOW TO STOP BEING
TOXIC WORKBOOK

A Proven Plan to End Dark Psychology, Master Emotional
Intelligence, Overcome Narcissism, and Build Strong
Relationships Without Hours of Therapy

Caleb Petersen

Table Of Contents

Buyer Bonus

As a special thank you for your purchase, I'm offering the HEALTHY RELATIONSHIPS TOOLKIT for FREE, exclusive to my readers! Visit the link or scan the QR code to download your free bonuses instantly.

emotionalhealingacademy.com/healthy-relationships-toolkit

Inside these bonuses, you'll discover:

- A clear, actionable guide for setting and maintaining boundaries that will transform your personal and professional relationships.
- The exact steps to follow for repairing relationships and restoring trust when things have gone wrong.
- The easiest tool to use so that you can reference anytime to track your progress in repairing relationships.
- The only quick-reference guide that is full of essential tips to boost your self-awareness and emotional intelligence, empowering you to manage your emotions more effectively.

If you **want to know how to set** and **maintain boundaries easily** and **effectively, the exact steps** to **follow** for **repairing relationships** and **restoring trust** when things go wrong, then grab your bonus.

INTRODUCTION

"If you don't heal what hurt you, you'll bleed on people who didn't cut you."

Let that sink in for a moment. It's a powerful truth bomb that gets to the heart of why you're holding this workbook right now. We've all been there—caught in a cycle of toxic behaviors, hurting the people we care about most, and feeling powerless to stop it. But here's the kicker: those toxic behaviors? They're not really about the people around us. They're about the wounds we carry, the pain we haven't processed, and the emotional baggage we've been lugging around.

You've picked up this workbook because something inside you knows it's time for a change. Maybe you've seen the hurt in your partner's eyes one too many times. Perhaps you've lost friends and can't figure out why. Or maybe you're just tired of feeling like you're your own worst enemy. Whatever brought you here, I want you to know something important: You've made the right choice.

This isn't just another self-help book that'll gather dust on your nightstand. It's not a collection of feel-good platitudes or quick fixes. What you're holding is a proven plan—a road map to help you break free from manipulative habits, master emotional intelligence, and achieve lasting change. This workbook is your first step toward creating the relationships and life you truly want and deserve.

Now, I can almost hear the skeptical voice in your head. "Yeah, right. I've tried to change before. It never sticks." I get it. Change is hard, and when you're dealing with deeply ingrained toxic behaviors, it can feel downright impossible. But here's the thing: You haven't had the right tools before. You haven't had a guide who's been in your shoes and found a way out.

That's where I come in. I'm not just some relationship guru spouting theories from an ivory tower. I've been where you are. I've felt the crushing weight of toxic patterns, the guilt of hurting loved ones, and the frustration of feeling stuck. As a relationship and conflict management coach, I've helped countless individuals break free from these destructive cycles. My methods aren't just feel-good fluff; they're rooted in personal experience, practical exercises, and solid research. I know they work because I've seen the transformations firsthand.

Let's get real for a moment: Toxic behaviors don't just appear out of nowhere. They're often coping mechanisms we developed to protect ourselves from pain, rejection, or vulnerability. Maybe you learned to manipulate situations to feel in control. Perhaps you use passive-aggressive tactics to express anger without risking confrontation, or you might push people away before they can get close enough to hurt you.

These behaviors might have served a purpose once, but now they're sabotaging your chances at genuine connection and happiness. The good news? You're not doomed to repeat these patterns forever. With the right tools and guidance, you can rewire your emotional responses and build healthier ways of relating to others and yourself.

In this workbook, we're going to dig deep. We'll explore the root causes of your toxic behaviors, shine a light on the emotional triggers that set you off, and develop strategies to interrupt those harmful patterns before they take over. You'll learn how to:

- Identify your specific toxic behaviors and understand their origins

- Develop emotional intelligence to better manage your feelings and reactions

- Communicate assertively without resorting to manipulation or aggression

- Set healthy boundaries that protect your well-being and respect others

- Cultivate empathy and vulnerability to build stronger, more authentic relationships

- Practice self-compassion to break the cycle of shame and self-sabotage

This isn't going to be a walk in the park. There will be moments when you want to throw this book across the room (please don't—papercuts are no joke). You'll face uncomfortable truths about yourself. You might cry. You might get angry. And that's okay. Real change isn't always comfortable, but I promise you it's worth it.

As we work through this book together, I want you to remember something crucial: You are not your toxic behaviors. Those patterns don't define you—they're simply habits you've learned. And anything learned can be unlearned and replaced with something better.

Think of this workbook as your personal emotional fitness program. Just like getting in physical shape, developing emotional intelligence and healthier relationship habits takes time and consistent effort. There will be days when you nail it and days when you stumble. The key is to keep showing up, doing the work, and trusting the process.

Self-awareness is one of the most powerful tools you'll develop through this workbook. It's like turning on a light in a dark room—suddenly, you can see what you're tripping over. As you become more aware of your patterns, triggers, and emotional responses, you'll gain the power to make different choices. You'll learn to pause in those critical moments between feeling and reacting, creating space for healthier responses.

But self-awareness alone isn't enough. That's why this workbook is packed with practical exercises, reflection prompts, and actionable strategies you can start using right away. We'll work on rewiring your thought patterns, developing new communication skills, and practicing emotional regulation techniques that will help you stay calm and centered even in challenging situations.

Remember, this isn't about becoming a perfect person (news flash: there's no such thing). It's about progress, not perfection. Every small step you take toward healthier behaviors is a victory worth celebrating. As you work through this book, be kind to yourself. Recognize that change takes time, and setbacks are part of the process.

You might be wondering, "Can I really change? Is it too late for me?" Let me be crystal clear: It is never too late to work on yourself and improve your relationships. Your past doesn't dictate your future unless you let it. Every day, every moment, is a new opportunity to make a different choice, respond with kindness instead of defensiveness, and reach for connection instead of pushing people away.

So, are you ready to start this journey? Ready to peel back the layers, face your fears, and emerge as a healthier, happier version of yourself? If you're nodding (or even if you're hesitating but still reading), then it's time to dive in.

Turn the page and take that first step toward transforming your toxic habits into healthy, emotionally intelligent behaviors. Your future self—and the people who love you—will thank you for it. Let's get started on creating the life and relationships you truly deserve.

SECTION 1

UNDERSTANDING YOUR EMOTIONAL TRIGGERS

Welcome to a crucial step in your journey toward overcoming toxic behaviors and cultivating healthier relationships. In this section, we'll dive deep into the complex world of emotional triggers—those powerful, often unconscious reactions that can drive our most problematic behaviors.

Understanding your emotional triggers is like decoding a personal mystery. It requires patience, courage, and a willingness to look beneath the surface of your actions to the deeper currents of emotion and experience that shape them. This exploration can be challenging, but it's also incredibly rewarding. As you uncover the roots of your toxic patterns, you'll gain the power to change them.

In the pages that follow, we'll embark on a three-part journey:

- First, we'll explore the profound link between past trauma and current toxic behaviors. You'll learn how unresolved pain from your past can shape your present actions, often in ways you might not even realize. Through real-world examples, you'll see how emotional wounds can manifest in manipulative or harmful patterns—and, more importantly, how understanding this connection is the first step toward healing.

- Next, we'll shine a light on the negative thought patterns that often drive toxic behaviors. These are the silent scripts running in the background of your mind, influencing your perceptions and reactions. You'll learn to recognize these patterns, challenge them, and ultimately rewrite them into more positive, constructive thoughts.

- Finally, we'll develop your skills in self-reflection and awareness. You'll learn to uncover the deeper roots of your behaviors through journaling prompts and targeted questions. You'll also discover how to map your behavior patterns across different relationships, revealing insights that can lead to profound personal growth.

This process is not about judgment or self-criticism. It's about understanding, acceptance, and growth. Every insight you gain is a step toward greater emotional freedom and healthier relationships.

As we begin, take a deep breath. Acknowledge the courage it takes to look within yourself this way. You're doing important work, and every step forward, no matter how small it might seem, is progress.

Let's start this journey of self-discovery together.

PART 1

IDENTIFYING THE ROOTS OF TOXICITY

Until you make the unconscious conscious, it will direct your life, and you will call it fate. –Carl Jung

Welcome to the first crucial step in your journey toward overcoming toxic behaviors and cultivating healthier relationships. In this chapter, we'll embark on an in-depth exploration of the emotional triggers that often lead to destructive patterns in our interactions with others and ourselves. By the time you finish this chapter, you'll have gained a profound understanding of where your toxic behaviors originate and how to begin addressing them at their very roots.

Understanding our emotional triggers is like decoding a complex puzzle. Each piece represents a part of our past experiences, thought patterns, and deeply ingrained beliefs. As we put these pieces together, we start to see the complete picture of our emotional landscape. This awareness is the foundational key to unlocking lasting change in our behaviors and relationships.

Remember, this process of self-discovery can be challenging. You may uncover painful memories or confront uncomfortable truths about yourself. But know this: Facing these challenges head-on is an act of immense courage and self-love. You're taking the first steps towards breaking free from toxic cycles and creating the fulfilling relationships you deserve.

Let's dive in and begin unraveling the intricate web of your emotional triggers.

The Link Between Past Trauma and Toxicity

Unraveling the Impact of Unresolved Trauma

Trauma, particularly childhood trauma, plays a significant role in shaping our adult behaviors. When we experience traumatic events, our brains develop coping mechanisms to protect us from further harm. These mechanisms, while initially protective, can evolve into toxic behaviors if left unaddressed.

To understand this better, let's explore the concept of the "wounded inner child." This psychological theory suggests that unresolved childhood issues continue to influence our adult behaviors. For instance, a child who experienced neglect might develop an intense fear of abandonment. As an adult, this fear could manifest in various toxic ways:

- **Clingy behavior**: Constantly seeking reassurance and attention from partners

- **Controlling tendencies**: Attempting to micromanage a partner's life to ensure they won't leave

- **Emotional manipulation**: Using guilt or threats to keep a partner close

It's crucial to understand that these behaviors, while harmful, often stem from a place of deep-seated pain and fear rather than malicious intent.

The Neuroscience of Trauma and Behavior

Recent neuroscientific research has shed light on how trauma affects our brain and, consequently, our behavior. Trauma can alter the functioning of the amygdala, the brain's emotional processing center, leading to heightened reactivity to perceived threats. This can result in:

- **Hypervigilance**: Always being on edge, expecting the worst in situations

- **Emotional dysregulation**: Difficulty managing intense emotions

- **Impaired impulse control**: Reacting without thinking, often in destructive ways

Understanding these neurological impacts can help us approach our behaviors with more compassion and insight.

Exercise: Mapping Your Trauma Response

Take a moment to reflect on your own experiences. Try to identify situations where you react strongly or in ways that seem disproportionate to the circumstance. These might be clues to underlying trauma responses.

1. Describe the situation:

_____

_____

_____

_____

2. Your emotional reaction:

_____

_____

_____

_____

3. Your behavioral response:

_____

_____

_____

_____

4. Can you link this to any past experiences?

_____

_____

_____

Repeat this exercise for 3-5 different situations. Look for patterns in your responses.

How Emotional Pain Manifests in Toxic Patterns

Emotional pain from past trauma often resurfaces in our current relationships, leading to toxic patterns. Let's explore some common manifestations in more depth:

- **Avoidance**

  o Manifestation: Pushing people away, fear of commitment, emotional unavailability.

  o Example: John, who was abandoned by his mother, finds himself unable to fully commit in relationships, always keeping an "escape route" open.

- **Overcompensation**

  o Manifestation: People-pleasing, neglecting own needs, losing sense of self in relationships.

  o Example: Emma, whose parents were highly critical, constantly goes out of her way to please her partner, often at the expense of her own well-being.

- **Projection**

  o Manifestation: Attributing own insecurities or negative traits onto others, paranoia.

  o Example: David, who struggles with fidelity, constantly accuses his partners of cheating, projecting his own tendencies onto them.

- **Gaslighting**

  o Manifestation: Manipulating others to doubt their own perceptions or memories.

  o Example: Lisa, who grew up with an alcoholic parent who denied their addiction, finds herself downplaying her own hurtful actions and making her partner question their reality.

- **Emotional Volatility**

  o Manifestation: Extreme mood swings, intense emotional reactions to minor triggers.

  o Example: Mike, who experienced unpredictable abuse as a child, has angry outbursts over minor inconveniences, scaring those around him.

Real-World Case Studies of Trauma-Based Behaviors

Let's delve deeper into some real-world examples to illustrate how past trauma can shape current behaviors:

Sarah's Story: The Test of Love

Sarah grew up with an emotionally absent father who eventually left the family. As an adult, Sarah found herself subconsciously "testing" her romantic partners. She would create conflicts or act distant, secretly hoping her partners would prove their love by fighting for the relationship. This behavior, rooted in her fear of abandonment, often pushed away the very people she longed to keep close.

- **Trauma Response**: Fear of abandonment leading to manipulative behavior

- **Toxic Pattern**: Creating unnecessary relationship drama as a test of loyalty

Mike's Experience: The Workplace Bully

Mike was severely bullied in school, leaving him with deep-seated insecurities about his worth and capabilities. In his adult life, Mike became known as the office bully. He would aggressively assert his opinions in meetings, belittle colleagues' ideas, and always need to "win" arguments. His behavior was an overcompensation for his childhood experiences, but it created a toxic work environment and hindered his career growth.

- **Trauma Response**: Insecurity and fear of being seen as weak or incapable

- **Toxic Pattern**: Aggressive behavior and need for dominance in workplace interactions

Lisa's Pattern: The Perfectionist Partner

Lisa's mother was highly critical and never satisfied with Lisa's achievements. As an adult, Lisa found herself being overly critical of her romantic partners. She would point out their flaws, criticize their efforts, and set unrealistic standards for the relationship. This behavior, stemming from her own fear of not being "good enough," often led to the breakdown of her relationships.

- **Trauma Response**: Internalized criticism and fear of imperfection

- **Toxic Pattern**: Excessive criticism and unrealistic expectations in relationships

Tom's Struggle: The Emotional Wall

Tom grew up in a household where expressing emotions was seen as a sign of weakness. His parents discouraged crying or showing vulnerability. As an adult, Tom struggled with emotional intimacy. He would shut down during emotional conversations, unable to express his feelings or empathize with his partner's emotions. This emotional unavailability created distance in his relationships and left his partners feeling unsupported and unloved.

- **Trauma Response**: Suppression of emotions and fear of vulnerability

- **Toxic Pattern**: Emotional unavailability and lack of empathy in relationships

Exercise: Identifying Your Trauma Responses

Now that we've explored several examples, let's turn the focus to your own experiences. This exercise will help you identify potential trauma responses in your behavior:

1. Think about a recent conflict or difficult situation in a relationship (romantic, familial, or friendship).

2. Describe the situation briefly.

3. What was your emotional reaction? Be as specific as possible about what you felt.

4. How did you behave in response to these emotions?

5. Reflect on your past experiences. Can you identify any similarities between this reaction and events from your past, particularly from childhood?

6. How might this reaction be a way of protecting yourself from past hurt?

---

7. What would a healthier response look like in this situation?

Repeat this exercise for 2-3 different situations. Look for patterns in your emotional reactions and behaviors. These patterns can provide valuable insights into your trauma responses and the roots of potentially toxic behaviors.

Remember, recognizing these patterns is not about blaming yourself or your past. It's about understanding the origins of your behaviors so you can begin to change them. Approach this exercise with self-compassion and curiosity.

Recognizing Negative Thought Patterns

Our thoughts play a crucial role in shaping our behaviors and emotional responses. Negative thought patterns, often deeply ingrained and automatic, can drive toxic behaviors in our relationships. By learning to recognize and challenge these patterns, we can begin to change our reactions and cultivate healthier interactions.

Common Negative Thought Patterns That Drive Toxic Behaviors

Let's explore some of the most common negative thought patterns in depth:

- **All-or-Nothing Thinking (Black-and-White Thinking)**

  o Description: Seeing things in absolute, binary terms with no middle ground.

  o Example: "If I'm not perfect, I'm a complete failure."

  o How it leads to toxic behavior: This thinking can lead to extreme reactions, unrealistic expectations of others, and an inability to compromise.

- **Overgeneralization**

  o Description: Taking one negative experience and applying it to all situations.

  o Example: "I got rejected once, so I'll always be rejected."

  o How it leads to toxic behavior: This can result in giving up easily, avoiding vulnerability, or preemptively pushing others away.

- **Mental Filter**

  o Description: Focusing solely on the negative aspects of a situation while filtering out all positive aspects.

  o Example: Fixating on one critical comment while ignoring multiple compliments.

  o How it leads to toxic behavior: This can lead to constant negativity, an inability to appreciate others, and creating a pessimistic atmosphere in relationships.

- **Jumping to Conclusions**

  o Description: Making negative interpretations without actual evidence. This includes mind-reading (assuming you know what others are thinking) and fortune-telling (predicting things will turn out badly).

  o Example: "They haven't texted back in an hour. They must be angry with me."

  o How it leads to toxic behavior: This can result in preemptive accusations, unnecessary arguments, and creating problems where none exist.

- **Catastrophizing**

  o Description: Always expecting the worst possible outcome in any situation.

  o Example: "If I make a mistake at work, I'll definitely get fired and end up homeless."

  o How it leads to toxic behavior: This can lead to excessive anxiety, controlling behaviors, and pushing others away with constant negativity.

- **Personalization**

  o Description: Believing that everything others do or say is a direct, personal reaction to you.

  o Example: "My friend seems distracted today. I must have done something to upset them."

  o How it leads to toxic behavior: This can result in taking things too personally, being overly defensive, and making situations about you when they're not.

- **"Should" Statements**

  o Description: Having rigid rules about how you and others "should" or "must" behave.

  o Example: "I should always be able to handle things on my own."

  o How it leads to toxic behavior: This can lead to unrealistic expectations, excessive self-criticism, and being overly judgmental of others.

- **Emotional Reasoning**

  o Description: Believing that if you feel something, it must be true.

  o Example: "I feel jealous, so my partner must be cheating on me."

  o How it leads to toxic behavior: This can result in acting on unfounded emotions, making accusations without evidence, and creating unnecessary conflict.

Exercise: Identifying Your Thought Patterns

Take a moment to reflect on your own thought patterns. For each of the negative thought patterns described above, try to identify a recent situation where you engaged in this type of thinking:

1. All-or-Nothing Thinking

_____

_____

_____

_____

_____

2.   Overgeneralization

3.   Mental Filter

4.   Jumping to Conclusions

5.   Catastrophizing

Caleb Petersen

6. Personalization

_____

_____

_____

7. "Should" Statements

_____

_____

_____

8. Emotional Reasoning

_____

_____

_____

How to Challenge and Rewrite These Harmful Thoughts

Recognizing negative thought patterns is the first step. The next crucial step is learning how to challenge and reframe these thoughts. Here's a detailed process for doing so:

1. **Identify the Thought**

   o Catch yourself in the moment of having a negative thought.

   o Write it down if possible.

2. Name the Thought Pattern

o Refer to the list above and try to identify which pattern this thought falls into.

o Understanding the type of thought can help you recognize it more quickly in the future.

3. Question the Evidence

o Ask yourself: "What evidence do I have that supports this thought?"

o Then ask: "What evidence do I have that doesn't support this thought?"

o Be as objective as possible, as if you were examining evidence in a court case.

4. Consider Alternative Perspectives

o Ask yourself: "How might someone else view this situation?"

o If a friend was in this situation, what advice would you give them?

5. Examine the Consequences

o Ask yourself: "What happens when I believe this thought?"

o "How does it affect my mood and behavior?"

o "Is holding onto this thought helpful or harmful to me?"

6. Generate Alternative Thoughts

o Based on the evidence and alternative perspectives, what are some other ways you could think about this situation?

o Try to come up with thoughts that are more balanced and realistic, not necessarily overly positive.

7. **Choose a Balanced Thought**

o Select the alternative thought that feels most true and helpful.

o It should acknowledge both the positives and negatives of the situation.

8. **Reinforce the New Thought**

o Repeat the new, balanced thought to yourself.

o Consider writing it down or setting it as a reminder on your phone.

Exercise: Challenging Your Thoughts

Let's practice this process with a specific example. Choose one negative thought you identified in the previous exercise. Work through the following steps:

1. The negative thought

_____

_____

_____

_____

2. The thought pattern this represents

_____

_____

_____

_____

3.   Evidence that supports this thought

4.   Evidence that doesn't support this thought

5.   How might someone else view this situation?

6.   What are the consequences of believing this thought?

7. Generate three alternative, more balanced thoughts

8. Choose the most realistic and helpful balanced thought

9. Write an affirmation based on this balanced thought that you can repeat to yourself

Remember, changing thought patterns takes time and practice. Be patient with yourself as you work through this process. With consistent effort, you'll find it becomes easier to catch and reframe negative thoughts.

Building Awareness Through Reflection

Self-reflection is a powerful tool for understanding our behaviors and emotions. By taking the time to introspect and analyze our thoughts and actions, we can gain valuable insights into our patterns and triggers. This awareness is crucial for making lasting changes in our behavior.

Journaling Prompts to Uncover the Roots of Toxic Behavior

Journaling can be an incredibly effective method for self-discovery and emotional processing. Here are some in-depth prompts to help you explore the roots of your toxic behaviors:

- **Childhood Experiences**

  o Describe your earliest memory of feeling hurt or betrayed. How did this experience make you feel? How do you think it has influenced your current relationships?

  _____

  _____

  _____

  _____

  o Write about your relationship with your primary caregivers during childhood. What patterns or dynamics do you notice? How might these have shaped your current behavior in relationships?

  _____

  _____

  _____

  _____

- **Relationship Patterns**

  o Think about your past romantic relationships. What common themes or issues do you notice? Are there patterns in how these relationships begin, progress, and end?

  o Describe a recent conflict in a relationship. What role did you play in this conflict? Can you identify any toxic behaviors you exhibited?

- **Emotional Reactions**

  o Recall a situation where you reacted much more strongly than the situation warranted. Describe the situation, your feelings, and your reaction in detail. What do you think triggered such an intense response?

  o What are your "emotional hot buttons"? What situations or behaviors from others tend to provoke strong emotional reactions in you?

- **Fear and Insecurity**

  o What are your biggest fears in relationships? Where do you think these fears come from?

  o Describe a time when you felt deeply insecure in a relationship. What triggered this insecurity? How did you behave as a result?

- **Coping Mechanisms**

  o How do you typically cope with stress or emotional pain? Are these methods healthy or potentially harmful?

o   Can you identify any behaviors you use to protect yourself emotionally? How might others perceive these behaviors?

- **Ideal vs. Reality**

o   Describe your ideal relationship. How does it differ from your current or past relationships?

o   What qualities do you value most in a partner? Do you embody these qualities yourself? If not, what holds you back?

- **Family Dynamics**

o Reflect on the relationship dynamics in your family of origin. Are there any patterns you've carried into your adult relationships?

o How were conflicts handled in your family growing up? How has this influenced your approach to conflict in your current relationships?

- **Self-Perception**

  o How do you think others perceive you in relationships? How does this compare to how you see yourself?

  _____

  _____

  _____

  _____

  o What aspects of yourself are you most critical of? How might this self-criticism manifest in your relationships?

  _____

  _____

  _____

  _____

Take your time with these prompts. You may want to focus on one or two per day, allowing yourself ample time for reflection and exploration. Remember, the goal is not to judge yourself but to understand yourself better.

Questions to Ask Yourself When Toxic Impulses Arise

Developing self-awareness in the moment when toxic impulses arise is crucial for changing our behaviors. Here's an expanded list of questions to ask yourself in these moments:

- **Emotion Identification**

  o What am I feeling right now? (Try to be as specific as possible.)

  o Where in my body do I feel this emotion?

  o On a scale of 1-10, how intense is this feeling?

- **Trigger Analysis**

  o What specific event or interaction triggered this feeling?

  _____

  _____

  _____

  o Has something similar happened before? How did I react then?

  _____

  _____

  _____

- **Thought Examination**

  o What thoughts are going through my mind right now?

  _____

  _____

  _____

  o Are these thoughts based on facts, or are they assumptions?

  _____

  _____

  _____

o   Which of the negative thought patterns we discussed earlier might these thoughts fall into?

- **Reaction Assessment**

o   Is my reaction proportionate to the situation?

o   How might my reaction impact others around me?

o   What would a healthier response look like?

- **Fear Exploration**

  o What am I afraid might happen in this situation?

  _____

  _____

  _____

  o Is this fear based on the current situation, or is it rooted in past experiences?

  _____

  _____

  _____

- **Need Identification**

  o What do I need right now? (e.g., reassurance, space, understanding)

  _____

  _____

  _____

  o Is there a way I can meet this need myself or communicate it effectively to others?

  _____

  _____

  _____

- **Alternative Perspectives**

  o How else could I interpret this situation?

  _____

  _____

  _____

  o If a friend were in this situation, what advice would I give them?

  _____

  _____

  _____

- **Consequence Consideration**

  o What might the short-term consequences be if I act on my current impulse?

  _____

  _____

  _____

  o What about the long-term consequences?

  _____

  _____

  _____

- **Past Pattern Recognition**

  o Have I been in a similar situation before? What happened when I reacted toxically?

  _____

  _____

  _____

  o Is there an opportunity here to break an old pattern?

  _____

  _____

  _____

- **Growth Opportunity**

  o What can I learn from this situation?

  _____

  _____

  _____

  o How can I use this as an opportunity for personal growth?

  _____

  _____

  _____

Practice asking yourself these questions when you feel triggered. Over time, this self-interrogation will become more natural and can help you pause before reacting toxically.

Mapping Behavior Patterns Across Relationships

Understanding how our behavior patterns manifest across different relationships can provide valuable insights into our core issues and triggers. This exercise will help you create a visual representation of your relationship dynamics.

Exercise: Creating Your Relationship Map

You'll need a large sheet of paper and different colored pens or markers for this exercise.

1. **Central Self**

   o In the center of the paper, draw a circle and write your name in it.

2. **Identify Key Relationships**

   o Around your central circle, draw smaller circles representing significant relationships in your life. Include family members, romantic partners (past and present), close friends, and even important professional relationships.

   o Connect each of these circles to your central circle with a line.

3. **Categorize Relationships**:

   o Use different colors to categorize these relationships (e.g., family in blue, romantic in red, friendships in green).

4. **Describe Dynamics**

   o Along each connecting line, write words or short phrases that describe the dynamic of that relationship. For example: "conflict-filled," "supportive," "distant," "intense," etc.

5. **Identify Common Issues**

o For each relationship, note any recurring issues or conflicts. Write these near the relevant circles.

6. **Your Typical Reactions**

o Next to each issue, jot down how you typically react. Be honest with yourself here.

7. **Outcomes**

o Finally, note the usual outcomes of these conflicts or issues.

8. **Look for Patterns**

o Step back and look at your completed map. Can you see any patterns?

o Are there common themes in how you react across different relationships?

o Do you see similar issues cropping up in multiple relationships?

9. **Reflect and Analyze**

o Now, answer the following questions:

   ■ What patterns do you notice in your relationships?

■ How might your reactions be contributing to these patterns?

■ Can you identify any core fears or beliefs that might be driving these patterns?

■ How do these patterns relate to your past experiences or family dynamics?

o   What changes would you like to make in these relationship dynamics?

_____

_____

_____

This visual mapping exercise can be a powerful tool for seeing the bigger picture of your relationship patterns. It may bring to light connections you hadn't noticed before and can serve as a roadmap for areas you'd like to work on.

Mindfulness Practice: Developing Real-Time Awareness

Mindfulness is a powerful tool for developing moment-to-moment awareness of our thoughts, feelings, and behaviors. This awareness is crucial for catching ourselves before we fall into toxic patterns. Here's a simple mindfulness exercise to help you develop this skill:

Exercise: The STOP Technique
Practice this technique several times a day, especially when you feel emotionally triggered:

- **S - Stop**: Whatever you're doing, just pause for a moment.

- **T - Take a breath**: Focus on your breath. Take a deep inhale and a slow exhale.

- **- Observe**: Notice what's happening inside you and around you:

o   What thoughts are going through your mind?

_____

_____

o   What emotions are you feeling? Where do you feel them in your body?

o   What's happening in your environment?

- **P - Proceed**: Move forward with awareness. How can you respond to this situation in a way that aligns with your values and goals?

By regularly practicing this technique, you'll develop the habit of pausing and checking in with yourself before reacting. This can be incredibly valuable in moments when you feel the urge to engage in toxic behaviors.

Understanding your emotional triggers is a journey of self-discovery and growth. Through exploring the link between past trauma and current behaviors, recognizing negative thought patterns, and building self-awareness through reflection, you've taken significant steps toward breaking free from toxic cycles.

Remember, this process takes time and patience. Be kind to yourself as you uncover potentially painful truths and work to change longstanding patterns. Every moment of awareness is a step toward healthier relationships and a more fulfilling life.

In the next chapter, we'll build on this foundation of self-awareness to start actively changing these patterns. We'll explore specific strategies for interrupting toxic behaviors and replacing them with healthier alternatives. Keep up the great work—you're already on the path to transformation!

Chapter Takeaways

- Past trauma, especially from childhood, can significantly influence our adult behaviors and relationship patterns.

- Common toxic behaviors often stem from deep-seated fears and unresolved emotional pain.

- Negative thought patterns like all-or-nothing thinking, overgeneralization, and catastrophizing can drive toxic behaviors.

- Challenging and reframing these thought patterns is key to changing our behaviors.

- Self-reflection through journaling and relationship mapping can provide valuable insights into our behavioral patterns.

- Developing real-time awareness through mindfulness can help us catch toxic impulses before acting on them.

Understanding our triggers and patterns is the crucial first step in the journey toward healthier relationships.

PART 2

TRANSFORMING NEGATIVE THOUGHT PATTERNS

Watch your thoughts, they become words; watch your words, they become actions; watch your actions, they become habits; watch your habits, they become character; watch your character, for it becomes your destiny. —Anonymous

Welcome to the next crucial step in your journey toward healthier relationships and personal growth. In our previous exploration, we uncovered the origins of our emotional triggers and learned to recognize negative thought patterns. Now, we're going to dive deep into the transformative process of reshaping these patterns.

Changing the way we think is a monumental but achievable task. Our thought patterns are often deeply ingrained, formed over years of experiences, and reinforced by habit. They're like well-worn paths in a forest—familiar and easy to follow. However, just as new paths can be forged through a forest, new neural pathways can be created in our brains. With consistent effort and the right strategies, it's possible to rewire our thinking and cultivate healthier mental habits.

In this chapter, we'll explore advanced techniques for challenging negative thoughts, delve into powerful cognitive restructuring methods, and equip you with a diverse toolbox of strategies to help you maintain positive thinking, even in the face of life's inevitable challenges. Remember, our goal isn't to eliminate negative thoughts entirely—that's neither realistic nor desirable. Instead, we're aiming to develop a more balanced, nuanced way of thinking that allows us to respond to life's ups and downs in healthier, more constructive ways.

Keep in mind that change takes time. Be patient with yourself. Each small step you take is progress, and even setbacks are opportunities for learning and growth. Let's begin this exciting phase of your personal evolution.

The Power of Cognitive Restructuring

Cognitive restructuring is a cornerstone technique in cognitive behavioral therapy (CBT), a widely respected and evidence-based approach to changing thought patterns and behaviors. At its core, cognitive restructuring involves identifying and actively changing negative thought patterns. It's based on the fundamental premise that our thoughts, feelings, and behaviors are all interconnected in a complex web of influence. By changing one element—in this case, our thoughts—we can create a ripple effect that positively impacts our emotions and behaviors.

The Thought-Emotion-Behavior Cycle

To truly harness the power of cognitive restructuring, it's crucial to understand the thought-emotion-behavior cycle. This cycle illustrates how our internal mental processes connect to our outward actions and experiences:

1. We encounter a situation or event in our environment.

2. Almost instantly, we have automatic thoughts about the situation. These thoughts are often so quick and habitual that we barely notice them.

3. These thoughts generate emotional responses. For example, if we interpret a situation as threatening, we might feel fear or anxiety.

4. Our emotions, in turn, influence our behaviors. If we're feeling anxious, we might avoid the perceived threat or react defensively.

5. Our behaviors then create new situations or alter our existing circumstances, which starts the cycle anew.

This cycle can be either virtuous or vicious, depending on the nature of our thoughts. Negative thought patterns can trap us in a downward spiral of adverse emotions and destructive behaviors. However, by intervening at the thought stage, we can positively influence our emotional states and behavioral responses, creating an upward spiral of well-being and healthier interactions.

Exercise: Mapping Your Thought-Emotion-Behavior Cycle

To make this concept more tangible, let's do a practical exercise. Think of a recent situation where you engaged in behavior you later regretted—perhaps a moment when you reacted with undue anger, withdrew from a meaningful interaction, or engaged in some form of self-sabotage.

Now, let's map out the cycle by jotting down the following:

1. **Situation**: Describe the event or circumstance that triggered the cycle. Be as specific as possible, noting relevant details about the setting, the people involved, and what was happening.

2. **Automatic Thoughts**: What went through your mind in that moment? Try to capture your unfiltered, immediate thoughts. These might be judgments, assumptions, predictions, or interpretations of the situation.

3. **Resulting Emotions**: What feelings arose as a result of these thoughts? Were you angry, sad, anxious, ashamed? Try to name the emotions as specifically as you can, and if possible, rate their intensity on a scale from 0-100.

_____

_____

_____

_____

_____

_____

4. **Behaviors**: How did you act in response to these emotions? What did you do or say? Include both your outward actions and any internal behaviors (like mentally shutting down or ruminating).

_____

_____

_____

_____

_____

5. **Consequences**: What was the outcome of your behavior? How did it impact the situation, the people around you, and your own state of mind?

_____

_____

_____

_____

_____

As you reflect on this cycle, where do you see opportunities for intervention? If you could go back to that moment, at which point would you choose to break the cycle? How might changing your thoughts have led to a different emotional response and, consequently, a different behavioral outcome?

This exercise illustrates the power of our thoughts in shaping our experiences and interactions. By becoming more aware of this cycle in action, we can start to identify crucial moments where we can intervene and make different choices.

Advanced Techniques for Challenging Negative Thoughts

Now that we've explored the thought-emotion-behavior cycle, let's dive into some advanced techniques for challenging and reframing negative thoughts. These strategies build upon the basic thought-challenging techniques we learned earlier, offering more nuanced and powerful ways to reshape our thinking patterns.

The Double-Standard Method

One of the most insidious aspects of negative thinking is how much harsher we often are on ourselves than we would be on others. The double-standard method helps us recognize and correct this imbalance.

Here's how it works: When you notice yourself engaging in harsh self-criticism, pause and ask yourself, "Would I say this to a close friend or loved one in the same situation?" More often than not, the answer is no. We tend to be much more understanding, forgiving, and supportive of others than we are of ourselves.

Exercise: Applying the Double-Standard

1. Think of a recent situation where you were very self-critical. It might be a mistake at work, a social faux pas, or a personal failure. Write down the situation and your self-critical thoughts.

2. Now, imagine a close friend or loved one was in the exact same situation. What would you say to them? How would you support and encourage them?

3. Compare your responses. What differences do you notice? Are you able to offer compassion, understanding, or practical advice to your friend that you withheld from yourself?

_____

_____

_____

4. The final step is to reframe your self-talk to be as kind and understanding as you would be to a friend. How can you rephrase your initial self-critical thoughts in a more compassionate, constructive way?

_____

_____

_____

_____

This exercise often reveals just how unnecessarily harsh we can be on ourselves. By consciously choosing to treat ourselves with the same kindness we extend to others, we can significantly reduce the emotional toll of our negative thoughts.

The Semantic Method

The words we use, even in our internal dialogue, can have a profound impact on our emotions and self-perception. The semantic method involves carefully examining and changing the language we use to describe situations and ourselves.

Often, our negative self-talk involves extreme, absolutist language: "always," "never," "completely," "terrible," "disaster." This kind of language amplifies our negative emotions and can make situations seem more dire than they really are.

Exercise: Reframing Your Language

1. Start by listing five negative self-statements you often think or say. These might be thoughts like "I'm a complete failure," "I always mess things up," or "Nobody likes me."

2. Now, let's rewrite each one using less extreme, more accurate language. The goal is not to sugar-coat reality but to describe situations and yourself in a more balanced, nuanced way.

For example:

- Instead of "I'm a complete failure," try "I made a mistake, but that doesn't define my whole self."

- Instead of "I always mess things up," consider "I sometimes make mistakes, like everyone does."

- Instead of "Nobody likes me," perhaps "I have some good friendships, and I'm working on building more connections."

As you practice this technique, pay attention to how the reframed statements feel compared to the original ones. Often, the revised versions feel more truthful and less emotionally charged, allowing us to approach situations with a clearer, calmer mindset.

The Continuum Method

Black-and-white thinking is a common cognitive distortion that can fuel negative thought patterns. The continuum method helps us challenge this all-or-nothing mentality by viewing thoughts and attributes on a spectrum rather than as absolutes.

Exercise: Creating a Continuum

1. Choose a negative self-belief you hold. It might be something like "I'm unlikeable," "I'm a failure," or "I'm incompetent."

2. Now, imagine this belief as a continuum or scale from 0 to 100. At 0, place the absolute worst-case scenario of this belief. At 100, place the absolute best-case scenario.

o For example, if your belief is "I'm unlikeable":

- 0 might be: "Everyone hates me, and I have no friends at all."

- 100 might be: "Everyone adores me, and I'm universally popular."

1. Now, consider where you actually fall on this continuum. What evidence can you find that places you somewhere between these extremes? Perhaps you have some good

56

friends or colleagues who enjoy working with you. Maybe you've received compliments or been invited to social events.

_____

_____

_____

_____

_____

By placing yourself on this continuum, you challenge the extreme negative belief and acknowledge the more complex reality of your situation. This can help reduce the emotional impact of the negative belief and open up possibilities for growth and change.

Cognitive Restructuring in Action

Now that we've explored some advanced techniques, let's put them into practice with a comprehensive cognitive restructuring exercise. This exercise, which we'll call the Thought Record 2.0, is an expanded version of the thought record we introduced earlier. It's a powerful tool for examining and reshaping our thought patterns in real-life situations.

The Thought Record 2.0

This exercise is particularly useful when you notice strong negative emotions or find yourself engaging in toxic behaviors. By working through this process, you can gain insight into your thought patterns and actively work to change them.

Here's how to complete the Thought Record 2.0:

1. **Situation**: Describe the event or circumstance that triggered your negative thoughts or emotions. Be as specific as possible about what happened, where you were, who was involved, and any other relevant details.

2. **Automatic Thoughts**: Write down the thoughts that went through your mind in response to the situation. These are often quick, reflexive thoughts that we barely notice. Try to capture them as accurately as possible without censoring or judging them.

3. **Emotions and Intensity**: Identify the emotions you felt as a result of these thoughts. Be as specific as you can in naming the emotions (e.g., "anxious" rather than just "bad"). Rate the intensity of each emotion on a scale from 0-100, where 0 is not at all and 100 is the most intense you've ever felt that emotion.

4. **Evidence For**: List any evidence that seems to support your automatic thoughts. Be objective here. What facts or observations appear to back up your initial interpretation of the situation?

5. **Evidence Against**: Now, challenge your automatic thoughts by looking for evidence that doesn't support them. Are there any facts you might be overlooking? Any alternative explanations for what happened?

6. **Alternative Thought**: Based on a balanced consideration of all the evidence, generate an alternative thought that is more realistic and helpful. This doesn't have to be overly positive—the goal is a balanced, nuanced perspective.

7. **Revised Emotion and Intensit**y: Reflect on how you feel after considering this alternative thought. Have your emotions changed? Rate the intensity of your emotions again on the 0-100 scale.

By working through this process, you're actively engaging in cognitive restructuring. You're challenging your automatic negative thoughts, considering alternative perspectives, and ultimately reshaping your emotional responses.

It's important to practice this technique regularly. Try completing this thought record for three different situations over the next week. As you become more familiar with the process, you may find that you can go through these steps mentally in challenging situations without needing to write everything down.

Maintaining Positive Thinking in Challenging Situations

Changing thought patterns in moments of calm reflection is one thing, but maintaining these changes in the face of real-life challenges is quite another. Life will inevitably present us with difficult situations, and it's in these moments that our new thinking skills are truly put to the test. Here are some strategies to help you maintain a more positive mindset even when facing adversity:

The ABCDE Model

This powerful model, developed by psychologist Albert Ellis, provides a structured approach to dealing with adversity. It's particularly useful in situations where you find yourself slipping back into negative thought patterns. The ABCDE model stands for:

A - Adversity: This is the challenging situation or event you're facing.

B - Beliefs: These are your thoughts or interpretations about the adversity.

C - Consequences: These are the emotional and behavioral results of your beliefs.

D - Dispute: This is where you challenge or question your beliefs.

E - Energization: This is the new outcome after disputing your beliefs.

Let's break this down with an example:

1. **Adversity**: You make a mistake at work, and your boss criticizes you in front of your colleagues.

2. **Beliefs**: "I'm incompetent. I'll probably get fired. Everyone thinks I'm a failure."

3. **Consequences**: You feel intense shame and anxiety. You withdraw from your colleagues and avoid taking on new projects.

4. **Dispute**: Challenge these beliefs. Is one mistake really proof of total incompetence? Is there any evidence that you might get fired, or is that an overreaction? Do you know for certain what others are thinking?

5. **Energization**: After disputing these beliefs, you might arrive at a new perspective: "I made a mistake, which is normal. This is an opportunity to learn and improve. I'll talk to my boss about how to do better next time."

By working through this model, you can transform a potentially demoralizing experience into an opportunity for growth and learning.

Positive Reframing

Positive reframing is a technique that involves finding the silver lining or learning opportunity in challenging situations. This doesn't mean denying the difficulty of a situation but choosing to focus on potential positive aspects or outcomes.

For example:

- A job loss could be reframed as an opportunity to explore new career paths.

- A relationship breakup might be seen as a chance for personal growth and to find a more compatible partner.

- A failure to achieve a goal could be viewed as valuable feedback on what to improve for next time.

The key to effective positive reframing is acknowledging the reality of the situation while actively looking for potential benefits or lessons. This can help reduce the emotional impact of negative events and maintain a more optimistic outlook.

Exercise: Finding the Silver Lining

Think of three recent negative experiences in your life. For each one, try to identify something positive that came out of it or a lesson you learned from the experience. This might be challenging at first, but with practice, it can become a powerful tool for maintaining a positive mindset in difficult times.

Gratitude Practice

Regular gratitude practice can profoundly affect our overall thought patterns. By intentionally focusing on the positive aspects of our lives, we can counterbalance our brain's natural tendency to fixate on the negative.

A simple yet effective way to cultivate gratitude is through a daily gratitude journal. Each day, write down three things you're grateful for. These can be big things (like supportive relationships or career achievements) or small daily pleasures (like a delicious meal or a beautiful sunset).

The key is to be specific and, when possible, to focus on different things each day. This encourages us to continually look for new sources of gratitude in our lives.

For example, instead of just writing, "I'm grateful for my friend," you might write, "I'm grateful for the supportive phone call I had with Emily today. Her words of encouragement really lifted my spirits."

By engaging in this practice regularly, you're training your brain to notice and appreciate positive aspects of your life. Over time, this can lead to a more positive overall outlook, making it easier to maintain optimistic thinking even in challenging situations.

Transforming negative thought patterns is a journey that requires consistent effort and practice. The techniques and exercises we've explored in this chapter provide you with a robust toolkit for challenging and reframing your thoughts. Remember, the goal isn't to eliminate all negative thoughts—that would be neither realistic nor desirable. Instead, we're aiming to develop a more balanced, nuanced way of thinking that allows us to respond to life's challenges in healthier, more constructive ways.

As you continue to practice these techniques, you'll likely find that your emotional reactions become less intense and your behaviors more aligned with your values and goals. This, in turn, will lead to healthier relationships and a greater sense of emotional well-being.

However, it's important to remember that this is an ongoing process. You may find that you make progress in some areas while still struggling in others. You might have days where these techniques come easily and others where you fall back into old patterns. This is all normal and part of the growth process.

The key is to approach this journey with patience, self-compassion, and persistence. Celebrate your successes, no matter how small they might seem. Learn from your setbacks, viewing them as opportunities for further growth rather than failures.

Chapter Takeaways

- Cognitive restructuring is a powerful tool for changing negative thought patterns.

- Advanced techniques like the double-standard method, semantic method, and continuum method can provide new perspectives on our thoughts.

- Regular practice with tools like the expanded thought record can help ingrain new thinking habits.

- Strategies like the ABCDE model, positive reframing, and gratitude practice can help maintain positive thinking in challenging situations.

- Changing thought patterns is an ongoing process that requires patience and consistent effort

PART 3

OVERCOMING PASSIVE-AGGRESSIVE COMMUNICATION

Passive-aggressive behavior is a form of covert anger. It is a way to punish or control others without having to take responsibility for it. –Dr. Scott Wetzler

Welcome to a pivotal chapter in your journey toward healthier relationships and more effective communication. Passive-aggressive behavior is a subtle yet destructive form of interaction that can erode trust, create misunderstandings, and foster a toxic environment. In this chapter, we'll explore passive aggression in depth, understand its roots, and, most importantly, develop strategies to overcome it.

As you work through this chapter, remember that change takes time and practice. Be patient with yourself, celebrate small victories, and keep pushing forward. Each exercise is designed to gradually build your awareness and skills. Take your time with each activity, reflecting deeply on your experiences and insights.

Let's begin this transformative journey together!

Recognizing Passive Aggression

Before we can change passive-aggressive behaviors, we need to be able to identify them. Passive aggression often masquerades as politeness or compliance while harboring underlying resentment or anger.

Read through the following scenarios. For each one, consider whether it demonstrates passive-aggressive behavior. Write your thoughts on why you believe it is or isn't passive-aggressive. This exercise will help you start recognizing the subtle signs of passive aggression in everyday interactions.

- sighing loudly when asked to do a task but agreeing to do it anyway

- politely declining an invitation to a party you don't want to attend

- saying, "Fine, whatever you want" during an argument, then giving the silent treatment

- forgetting to do a promised favor repeatedly

- expressing disappointment directly when a friend cancels plans

- making sarcastic comments about a coworker's idea in a meeting

- asking for clarification on a task you don't understand

- procrastinating on a project to frustrate your boss

Now, reflect on a recent interaction where you felt frustrated or angry but didn't express it directly. Describe the situation, how you behaved, and what emotions you were feeling underneath. Then, consider what a more direct way to handle the situation might have been. This reflection will help you start identifying your own passive-aggressive tendencies and imagine alternatives.

The Emotional Roots of Passive Aggression

Understanding why we resort to passive-aggressive behavior is crucial for changing it. Consider each of the following potential root causes of passive-aggression. For each one, try to recall a personal example of when you might have acted passive-aggressively for this reason. Describe the situation, your behavior, and how the root cause influenced your actions.

1. Fear of conflict

2. Low self-esteem

3. Feeling powerless

4. Unexpressed anger

5. Learned behavior from family

6. Fear of abandonment

After exploring each root cause, reflect on which one resonates most with you. How has it influenced your communication style in your relationships? This deeper understanding of your motivations will be valuable as we work on changing these patterns.

The Impact of Passive Aggression

Passive-aggressive behavior can have far-reaching consequences on our relationships and overall well-being. Let's explore these impacts to motivate our journey toward more direct communication.

Think of a specific time when you behaved passive-aggressively. Describe the situation in detail, including:

1. What happened

_____

_____

_____

2. Your passive-aggressive behavior

_____

_____

_____

3. The immediate consequences

_____

_____

_____

4. The long-term impact on the relationship

_____

_____

_____

5.   How you felt afterward

_____

_____

_____

_____

_____

6.   How you think the other person might have felt

_____

_____

_____

_____

_____

Now, imagine how the outcome might have been different if you had communicated directly instead. What could you have said or done differently? How might the other person have responded?

Next, recall a time when someone else behaved passive aggressively toward you. Describe:

1. The situation

2. Their passive-aggressive behavior

3. How it made you feel

4. How it affected your relationship with that person

5. How you wish they had communicated instead

Reflect on how being on the receiving end of passive-aggression has influenced your own communication style. Has it made you more likely to use passive-aggressive communication yourself, or has it motivated you to communicate more directly?

Tools for Direct Communication

Now that we understand passive-aggression better, let's focus on developing tools for more direct, assertive communication.

Emotional Awareness Exercise

For the next week, set three random alarms on your phone each day. When the alarm goes off, pause and answer these questions:

1. What am I feeling right now?

---

2. Where do I feel this emotion in my body?

_____

_____

_____

_____

3. What triggered this emotion?

_____

_____

_____

4. How would I express this feeling directly?

_____

_____

_____

_____

Keep a log of your responses. At the end of the week, review your log and consider:

- What patterns do you notice in your emotional responses?

- Were there any emotions that were particularly challenging to identify or express?

- How has this exercise changed your awareness of your emotions?

This practice will help you become more attuned to your emotions in real time, a crucial skill for direct communication.

Crafting "I" Statements

"I" statements are a powerful tool for expressing feelings without blame. Practice converting the following passive-aggressive statements into "I" statements using this format:

"I feel [emotion] when [situation] because [reason]. I need/would like [request]."

- "Great, thanks for showing up on time as usual."

- "Don't worry about me; I'll just sit here alone while you go out and have fun."

- "I guess my opinion doesn't matter around here."

After crafting your "I" statements, reflect on how it feels to express yourself this way compared to using passive-aggressive comments. What challenges did you face in crafting these statements?

_____

_____

_____

_____

Assertiveness Role-Play Exercise

This exercise is designed to help you practice assertiveness techniques. There are multiple ways to approach this, depending on your situation:

Option 1: With a Partner

If you have a trusted friend, family member, or therapist willing to practice with you:

1. Choose who will play the frustrated roommate and who will play the roommate who leaves dishes.

2. Act out the scenario, focusing on these assertiveness techniques:

o Use a calm, clear voice.

o Maintain eye contact.

o   Keep your body language open and confident.

o   State your needs or opinions clearly and respectfully.

o   Be willing to compromise and find mutually beneficial solutions.

3. Switch roles and repeat the exercise.

Option 2: Solo Practice

If you're working through this book on your own:

1. Find a mirror or use your phone's camera in selfie mode.

2. Play both roles yourself, speaking out loud.

3. When playing the frustrated roommate, focus on using assertive body language and tone.

4. When playing the other roommate, practice listening and responding.

Option 3: Imaginary Dialogue

If you prefer not to speak out loud or use a mirror:

1. Write out the dialogue as a script, including notes about tone and body language.

2. Include lines for both the frustrated roommate and the one who leaves dishes.

3. Focus on crafting assertive statements and respectful responses.

How To Stop Being Toxic

Option 4: With a Therapist

If you're working through this book with a therapist:

1. Discuss the scenario with your therapist and decide who will play each role.

2. Use the session time to practice the role-play, with your therapist providing feedback.

3. Discuss how you might apply these skills in real-life situations.

Scenario

Your roommate frequently leaves dirty dishes in the sink.

Reflection Questions

After completing the exercise (in whichever format you chose), reflect on these questions:

1. How did it feel to communicate assertively?

2. What was challenging about this interaction?

3. How was this different from how you might have handled it in the past?

4. If you practiced alone, what insights did you gain from playing both roles?

5. How might you adapt these techniques for use in real-life situations?

Remember, the goal is to practice and become comfortable with assertive communication. It may feel awkward at first, but with practice, these skills will become more natural. If you're working through this alone, consider recording your practice sessions (audio or video) to review and track your progress.

Putting It All Together

Now, it's time to apply everything we've learned to real-life scenarios.

Communication Makeover

For each of the following scenarios, write out a passive-aggressive response. Then, rewrite it as a direct, assertive communication using the tools we've practiced.

- Your partner is consistently late when you have plans together.

- Your coworker consistently leaves their share of a project for you to complete.

- Your friend makes plans that you're not comfortable with, but you agree to go along with it.

After completing this exercise, reflect on which scenario was the most challenging to reframe and why you think that is.

Real-Life Application

Over the next week, commit to replacing passive-aggressive communication with direct, assertive communication in your daily life. Keep a journal of your experiences, noting:

1. The situation

2. Your initial passive-aggressive impulse

3. How you chose to communicate instead

4. The outcome of the interaction

5. How you felt afterward

At the end of the week, reflect on your experiences:

- What changes did you notice in your interactions?

- How did others respond to your more direct communication?

- What challenges did you face, and how did you overcome them?

- What benefits did you experience from communicating more directly?

Chapter Takeaways

Congratulations on completing this chapter! You've taken important steps toward understanding passive-aggressive behavior and developing healthier communication habits. Remember, changing long-standing patterns takes time and practice. Be patient with yourself and keep applying these tools in your daily life.

As you continue your journey, keep these key takeaways in mind:

- Passive-aggressive behavior often stems from fear of conflict, feelings of powerlessness, or unexpressed emotions.

- The impact of passive aggression on relationships can be significant and long-lasting.

- Emotional awareness is key to replacing passive-aggressive tendencies with direct communication.

- "I" statements, assertiveness techniques, and practicing empathy are powerful tools for more effective communication.

- Changing communication patterns takes time and consistent effort, but the benefits to your relationships and well-being are substantial.

Coming up, we'll build on these skills to tackle conflict resolution, using our new assertive communication techniques to navigate disagreements more effectively. Keep up the great work!

SECTION 2

THE DETOX PLAN - ELIMINATING TOXIC HABITS

This section may be one of the most challenging yet potentially transformative parts of our exploration. It requires courage, honesty, and a willingness to confront uncomfortable truths. However, it is through this process that we open the door to genuine change and healing.

In the pages that follow, we will explore three crucial aspects of facing the consequences of toxicity:

First, we'll examine the impact on others. Here, we'll delve into how toxic behavior erodes trust and intimacy in our relationships. We'll look at real stories of relationships affected by manipulation, providing a mirror through which we might recognize our own patterns. Most importantly, we'll confront the emotional toll our toxic behavior takes on our loved ones, cultivating empathy and understanding that can motivate our journey toward change.

Next, we'll turn our attention inward to the toll on mental health. We'll explore how engaging in toxic behaviors doesn't just harm others but also exacts a heavy price on our own well-being. We'll examine the guilt, anxiety, and depression that often accompany toxic patterns and understand why unchecked behavior can spiral into deeper emotional issues. Crucially, we'll also discover tools for coping with the mental burden of toxic habits, providing a lifeline as we navigate this challenging terrain.

We'll also tackle accountability and acknowledgment. This section forms the bridge between understanding our toxic behaviors and actively working to change them. We'll learn why accepting responsibility is not just important but crucial for real change. Through exercises in acknowledging the harm we've caused, we'll develop a deeper understanding of the impact of our actions. We'll also explore inspiring examples of how accountability can lead to emotional healing, offering hope and a roadmap for our own journeys.

As we navigate these topics, it's important to remember the role that dark psychology and narcissism can play in toxic behaviors. While not all toxic behavior stems from narcissism or intentional manipulation, understanding these deeper psychological patterns can shed light on some of the more insidious aspects of toxicity. We'll explore how traits associated with narcissism, such as lack of empathy and manipulative tendencies, can amplify the harmful effects of toxic behaviors. Additionally, we'll discuss how awareness of dark psychology techniques can help us recognize and counteract manipulative patterns in ourselves and others. This knowledge will serve as a crucial tool in our journey toward healthier relationships and authentic personal growth.

It's essential to approach this stage of the journey with self-compassion. Facing the consequences of our actions can be painful, but remember that this pain is a sign of growth. It indicates an expanding awareness and a deepening capacity for empathy and responsibility.

This process isn't about shame or self-flagellation. Instead, it's about honest self-reflection, making amends where possible, and committing to a path of personal growth and positive change. By facing these consequences head-on, we can create the possibility for profound transformation—in ourselves, in our relationships, and in the ripple effect we have on the world around us.

Remember, the fact that you're engaging with this material shows great courage and a desire for meaningful change. As we move through these challenging topics, be patient with yourself. Healing and growth take time, but every step forward, no matter how small, is progress.

Let's begin this crucial phase of our journey together with open hearts and minds, ready to face the truth and embrace the potential for change.

PART 1

THE IMPACT OF TOXIC BEHAVIOR ON OTHERS

In our journey to overcome toxic behaviors, it's crucial to understand not just how these behaviors affect us but also the profound impact they have on those around us. This section will explore the ripple effects of toxicity in relationships, examining how trust and intimacy are eroded, sharing real stories of manipulation, and delving into the emotional toll on our loved ones.

How Toxic Behavior Erodes Trust and Intimacy

Trust and intimacy are the bedrock of healthy relationships. They create a safe space where we can be vulnerable, express our true selves, and grow together. However, toxic behaviors can chip away at this foundation, sometimes so gradually that we don't notice until the damage is severe.

The Slow Decay of Trust

Trust is built through consistent, reliable behavior over time. It's a delicate balance of expectations and fulfillment. When we engage in toxic behaviors, we're essentially breaking the implicit agreements in our relationships. Here's how different toxic behaviors can erode trust:

- **Lying and Deception**: Even small lies can create doubt. When we're dishonest, we're telling our loved ones that we don't trust them with the truth. Over time, they learn they can't trust our words or actions.

- **Manipulation**: When we use guilt, gaslighting, or other manipulative tactics, we're prioritizing our desires over the well-being of others. This breeds resentment and suspicion.

- **Inconsistency**: Hot-and-cold behavior, where we're loving one moment and distant the next, creates uncertainty. Our loved ones never know which version of us they'll encounter.

- **Breaking Promises**: Repeatedly failing to follow through on commitments shows that our word can't be relied upon.

- **Invasion of Privacy**: Snooping through a partner's phone or personal belongings signals that we don't trust them, which paradoxically makes them trust us less.

The Withering of Intimacy

Intimacy goes beyond physical closeness. It's about emotional connection, vulnerability, and mutual understanding. Toxic behaviors can create barriers to intimacy in several ways:

- **Emotional Walls**: When we're consistently hurtful or untrustworthy, our loved ones may build emotional defenses to protect themselves.

- **Fear of Vulnerability**: If sharing feelings leads to criticism or manipulation, people learn to keep their thoughts and emotions to themselves.

- **Lack of Emotional Safety**: Constant criticism or mood swings create an environment where others don't feel safe expressing themselves.

- **Decreased Physical Intimacy**: In romantic relationships, emotional distance often translates to physical distance.

- **Loss of Shared Experiences**: As relationships become strained, we may spend less quality time together, further reducing opportunities for intimacy.

Exercise: Reflecting on Trust and Intimacy

Take a moment to reflect on your own relationships:

1. Think of a time when someone's behavior eroded your trust in them. How did it make you feel? How did it change your behavior toward them?

2. Now, consider a time when you might have engaged in behavior that eroded someone's trust in you. What were the consequences? How did it affect your relationship?

3. In your closest relationship, how would you rate the level of intimacy on a scale of 1-10? What factors contribute to this rating? Are there any toxic behaviors that might be hindering deeper intimacy?

Stories of Relationships Affected by Manipulation

Looking at real-life examples is helpful for truly understanding the impact of toxic behaviors. The following stories, with names changed for privacy, illustrate how manipulation can affect different types of relationships.

Sarah and John: The Slow Burn of Gaslighting

Sarah and John had been married for five years when Sarah started to notice changes in their relationship. John often made plans without consulting her, and when she brought it up, he'd insist they had discussed it. "You must have forgotten," he'd say, "You've been so forgetful lately."

At first, Sarah doubted herself. Maybe she was being forgetful, but as time went on, she noticed this pattern extending to other areas of their life. John would deny saying hurtful things, claim Sarah had agreed to decisions she hadn't been part of, and frequently tell her she was overreacting or being too sensitive.

Sarah's confidence began to crumble. She second-guessed her own memory and perceptions. She felt anxious and depressed, always walking on eggshells to avoid upsetting John. Their once-loving relationship had turned into a source of stress and self-doubt for Sarah.

It wasn't until Sarah confided in a close friend that she began to see John's behavior for what it was: gaslighting. This manipulative tactic had slowly eroded Sarah's sense of reality and self-worth, damaging the trust and intimacy in their marriage.

The Martinez Family: The Ripple Effect of Guilt-Tripping

The Martinez family had always been close-knit, but things changed when the oldest son, Miguel, moved to another city for work. His mother, Elena, struggled with the separation and began using guilt as a way to maintain control.

"If you really cared about this family, you'd visit more often," she'd say during their phone calls. "I guess your new friends are more important than your parents now."

Miguel felt torn. He loved his family but also valued his independence and new life. Each call with his mother left him feeling guilty and stressed. He began to dread their conversations and started calling less frequently to avoid the emotional manipulation.

The guilt-tripping didn't just affect Miguel. His younger sister, Lucia, who still lived at home, felt pressured to compensate for Miguel's absence. She put her own life on hold, afraid to pursue opportunities that might take her away from home.

Over time, the once-warm family dynamics became strained. Family gatherings were tense, with unspoken resentments simmering beneath the surface. Elena's manipulation, born out of her own fears and insecurities, was pushing away the very people she was trying to keep close.

Mark and His Colleagues: The Workplace Manipulator

Mark was known as a charismatic and successful team leader in his office, although those who worked closely with him saw a different side. Mark had a habit of taking credit for his team's ideas and deflecting blame when things went wrong.

He charmed upper management while subtly undermining his colleagues. "Great idea," he'd say in meetings. It's similar to what I suggested to Alissa last week. Glad you ran with it, Alissa." Alissa, caught off guard, would be left questioning her own memory of events.

When projects faced challenges, Mark was quick to point fingers. "If only Alex had completed his part on time," he'd say, neglecting to mention the unrealistic deadlines he had set.

Over time, team morale plummeted. Trust among colleagues eroded as they became wary of sharing ideas. A culture of suspicion and self-preservation replaced the collaborative spirit that had once made the team successful.

Productivity suffered, and eventually, valuable team members started looking for jobs elsewhere. Mark's manipulative behavior had not only hurt individuals but had also poisoned the entire work environment.

Reflection Questions

After reading these stories, take a moment to reflect:

1. Can you identify with any of the characters in these stories? Have you been in a similar situation, either as the person engaging in manipulation or on the receiving end?

2. What patterns of manipulative behavior do you notice across these stories?

3. How did the manipulation in each story affect not just the primary relationship but also the broader network of relationships?

4. If you were to advise the people in these stories, what would you say? What steps could they take to address the manipulation in their relationships?

_____

_____

_____

The Emotional Toll Toxic Behavior Takes on Loved Ones

While the stories above illustrate some of the ways toxic behavior can play out in relationships, it's important to delve deeper into the emotional impact on those on the receiving end. The effects of prolonged exposure to toxic behavior can be profound and long-lasting.

Erosion of Self-Esteem

One of the most significant impacts of toxic behavior is the gradual erosion of self-esteem in those subjected to it. This can manifest in several ways:

- **Self-Doubt**: Constant criticism or gaslighting can lead individuals to question their own judgment, abilities, and even their perception of reality.

- **Feelings of Inadequacy**: Repeated put-downs or impossibly high standards set by a toxic individual can lead to a pervasive sense of not being "good enough."

- **Loss of Identity**: In an effort to please a toxic individual or avoid conflict, people may suppress their own personalities, losing touch with who they really are.

Anxiety and Depression

Living with toxic behavior can take a serious toll on mental health:

- **Constant Stress**: The unpredictability of a toxic person's moods or actions can lead to a state of hypervigilance, where individuals are always on edge, waiting for the next outburst or manipulation.

- **Feelings of Hopelessness**: As the relationship deteriorates, individuals may feel trapped and unable to see a way out, leading to depression.

- **Anxiety in Other Relationships**: The fear and insecurity bred in a toxic relationship can spill over, causing anxiety in other relationships and social situations.

Physical Health Impacts

The stress of dealing with toxic behavior doesn't just affect mental health; it can have physical manifestations as well:

- **Sleep Disturbances**: Anxiety and stress can lead to insomnia or poor sleep quality.

- **Weakened Immune System**: Chronic stress can suppress the immune system, leading to more frequent illnesses.

- **Stress-Related Health Issues**: Conditions like high blood pressure, digestive problems, and chronic pain can be exacerbated by the stress of toxic relationships.

Impact on Other Relationships

The effects of a toxic relationship often ripple out, affecting other relationships in a person's life:

- **Social Isolation**: Toxic individuals often seek to isolate their victims from friends and family, leading to a shrinking social circle.

- **Difficulty in Trusting Others**: After experiencing manipulation and betrayal, individuals may find it hard to trust in new relationships.

- **Replication of Toxic Patterns**: Sometimes, people who have been in toxic relationships unconsciously replicate those patterns in other relationships, perpetuating the cycle.

Long-Term Emotional Scars

Even after a toxic relationship ends, the emotional impact can linger:

- **Trauma Bonds**: The intense highs and lows of a toxic relationship can create a strong emotional bond that's hard to break, even when the relationship is clearly unhealthy.

- **PTSD-Like Symptoms**: In severe cases, individuals may experience symptoms similar to post-traumatic stress disorder, including flashbacks and severe anxiety.

- **Difficulty With Intimacy**: The betrayal of trust in a toxic relationship can make it challenging to be vulnerable and intimate in future relationships.

Exercise: Recognizing the Impact

Take a moment to reflect on how toxic behavior has affected you or someone close to you:

1. Think of a relationship (past or present) where toxic behavior was present. What emotions do you associate with this relationship?

---

2. How did this relationship affect your:

o self-esteem?

o mental health?

o physical health?

o other relationships?

3. If you've left a toxic relationship, what lingering effects have you noticed? How have you worked to heal from these?

4. If you recognize that you've engaged in toxic behaviors, how do you think it has affected those close to you? Try to put yourself in their shoes and describe the emotional impact.

The Ripple Effect of Toxicity

As we've explored in this section, the impact of toxic behavior extends far beyond the immediate interaction. It creates a ripple effect, touching every aspect of a person's life and often spreading to affect a wider circle of relationships.

Understanding this impact is a crucial step in breaking the cycle of toxic behavior. Whether you've been on the receiving end of toxicity or recognize toxic patterns in your own behavior, acknowledging the far-reaching consequences is the first step toward change.

Remember, recognizing these patterns doesn't make you a bad person. We all have the capacity for toxic behavior, often born out of our pain or learned responses. The key is to take responsibility for our actions and their impact on others.

As we move forward, we'll explore strategies for healing from toxic relationships and developing healthier patterns of interaction. But for now, sit with this understanding. Let it motivate you to make positive changes, not out of guilt but out of a genuine desire to create healthier, more fulfilling relationships for yourself and those around you.

PART 2

THE TOLL ON MENTAL HEALTH FROM TOXIC BEHAVIORS

As we continue our journey of understanding and overcoming toxic behaviors, it's crucial to examine the profound impact these patterns can have on our mental health. This section will explore the psychological consequences of engaging in toxic behaviors, the potential for escalation if left unchecked, and provide tools for coping with the mental burden these habits create.

Guilt, Anxiety, and Depression as Consequences of Toxic Patterns

Engaging in toxic behaviors doesn't just harm our relationships; it can also take a significant toll on our mental well-being. Let's explore three common psychological consequences: guilt, anxiety, and depression.

The Weight of Guilt

Guilt is often the first emotional response we experience after engaging in toxic behavior. It's our conscience telling us that our actions have caused harm or violated our personal values.

- **Rational Versus Irrational Guilt**: Rational guilt can be a helpful emotion, motivating us to make amends and change our behavior. However, toxic patterns often lead to irrational guilt, where we excessively blame ourselves, even for things beyond our control.

- **The Guilt-Shame Spiral**: Unaddressed guilt can evolve into shame. While guilt says, "I did something bad," shame says, "I am bad." This shame can fuel further toxic behaviors as a misguided attempt to protect our fragile self-image.

- **Impact on Self-Esteem**: Chronic guilt erodes self-esteem, making us feel unworthy of love and respect. This can create a spiraling self-fulfilling prophecy, where we act in ways that push others away, confirming our negative self-perception.

Exercise: Examining Your Guilt

Take a moment to reflect on your feelings of guilt:

1. Identify a recent situation where you felt guilty about your behavior.

_____

_____

_____

_____

2. Was this guilt rational (proportionate to the situation) or irrational (excessive)?

_____

_____

_____

_____

3. How did this guilt affect your subsequent behavior and thoughts about yourself?

_____

_____

_____

_____

4. If the guilt was rational, what steps could you take to make amends or change your behavior?

_____

_____

_____

_____

5. If the guilt was irrational, how can you reframe your thoughts more realistically?

_____

_____

_____

_____

The Grip of Anxiety

Toxic behaviors often stem from and contribute to anxiety. This can create a vicious cycle that's hard to break.

- **Anticipatory Anxiety**: We may experience anxiety about potential conflicts or the consequences of our actions, leading to avoidance or more toxic behaviors as a misguided form of self-protection.

- **Social Anxiety**: Toxic patterns can damage our relationships, leading to increased anxiety in social situations. We may worry about how others perceive us or fear rejection.

- **Generalized Anxiety**: Over time, the stress of maintaining toxic patterns can contribute to a persistent state of worry and tension that permeates all aspects of life.

- **Physical Symptoms**: Chronic anxiety can manifest physically as headaches, digestive issues, muscle tension, and sleep disturbances.

Exercise: Anxiety Awareness
For the next week, keep an anxiety journal:

1. Each day, note situations where you feel anxious.

2. Rate the intensity of your anxiety on a scale of 1-10.

3. Identify any toxic behaviors you engaged in before, during, or after feeling anxious.

4. Reflect on how these behaviors might be contributing to or resulting from your anxiety.

At the end of the week, review your journal. What patterns do you notice? How might breaking toxic behavior patterns help reduce your anxiety?

The Descent Into Depression

Prolonged engagement in toxic behaviors can contribute to the development or exacerbation of depression.

- **Loss of Pleasure**: As toxic patterns damage our relationships and self-esteem, we may find less joy in activities we once enjoyed.

- **Isolation**: Toxic behaviors often lead to social withdrawal, either because others distance themselves from us or because we isolate ourselves out of shame or fear.

- **Negative Self-Talk**: The shame and guilt associated with toxic behaviors can fuel a pattern of negative self-talk, a key feature of depression.

- **Learned Helplessness**: Repeated failed attempts to change toxic patterns can lead to a sense of helplessness, a belief that we're incapable of change.

- **Cognitive Distortions**: Depression can reinforce the cognitive distortions that often underlie toxic behaviors, creating a self-perpetuating cycle.

Exercise: Challenging Negative Self-Talk

Identify three negative statements you often tell yourself related to your toxic behaviors. For each statement:

1. Write down the negative statement.

2. Identify the cognitive distortion at play (e.g., all-or-nothing thinking, overgeneralization, catastrophizing).

3. Challenge the thought with evidence to the contrary.

_____

_____

_____

4. Create a more balanced, realistic statement.

_____

_____

_____

Here's an example:

1. Negative statement: "I always ruin relationships. I'm unlovable."

2. Cognitive distortion: Overgeneralization, all-or-nothing thinking

3. Challenge: I have had positive relationships in the past. People have expressed love for me.

4. Balanced statement: "I've made mistakes in relationships, but I'm capable of love and being loved. I can learn and grow from my experiences."

Why Unchecked Behavior Can Spiral Into Deeper Emotional Issues

When left unaddressed, toxic behaviors don't just persist – they often escalate, leading to more severe emotional and psychological issues. Understanding this progression can motivate us to take action and seek help when needed.

The Cycle of Emotional Dysregulation

1. **Trigger**: An event or situation activates our emotional vulnerabilities.

2. **Emotional Response**: We experience intense emotions, often disproportionate to the trigger.

3. **Toxic Behavior**: Unable to regulate our emotions healthily, we engage in toxic behavior as a maladaptive coping mechanism.

4. **Consequences**: Our behavior damages relationships and self-esteem.

5. **Increased Vulnerability**: The negative consequences make us more sensitive to future triggers.

6. **Repeat**: The cycle begins again, often with increased intensity.

The Role of Neuroplasticity

- Our brains are remarkably adaptable, constantly forming new neural connections based on our experiences and behaviors. This neuroplasticity can work for or against us:

- **Reinforcing Negative Patterns**: Each time we engage in toxic behavior, we strengthen the neural pathways associated with that behavior, making it more likely we'll repeat it in the future.

- **Emotional Sensitivity**: Repeated exposure to stress and negative emotions can make our brains more sensitive to negative stimuli, lowering our threshold for emotional reactions.

- **Impaired Emotion Regulation**: Chronic stress from toxic patterns can impact the prefrontal cortex, the area of the brain responsible for emotional regulation and decision-making.

Exercise: Recognizing Escalation

Reflect on your own experiences with toxic behaviors:

1. Think of a toxic behavior you've engaged in. How has this behavior changed over time? Has it become more frequent or intense?

2. Have you noticed an increase in your emotional sensitivity or reactivity?

3. Are there any signs that your toxic patterns might be contributing to more severe emotional issues?

4. If you're comfortable doing so, share your reflections with a trusted friend or therapist. Sometimes, others can provide valuable insights into patterns we might not see ourselves.

Tools for Coping With the Mental Burden of Toxic Habits

Recognizing the impact of toxic behaviors on our mental health is an essential first step. Now, let's explore some practical tools and strategies for coping with and ultimately changing these patterns.

Mindfulness and Self-Awareness

Mindfulness is the practice of being present and fully engaged with whatever we're doing at the moment. Mindfulness activities can include coloring, completing a word search, doodling, completing puzzles, and more. It can be a powerful tool for breaking toxic patterns:

- **Mindful Breathing**: When you feel overwhelmed, take a few minutes to focus on your breath. This can help interrupt the cycle of toxic thoughts and behaviors.

- **Body Scan**: Regularly check in with your body. Where are you holding tension? How does your body feel before, during, and after engaging in toxic behaviors?

- **Emotion Labeling**: Practice identifying and naming your emotions. This simple act can help reduce their intensity and give you more control over your responses.

Exercise: Daily Mindfulness Check-In
For the next week, set aside five minutes each day for a mindfulness check-in:

1. Find a quiet place and sit comfortably.

2. Take three deep breaths, focusing on the sensation of breathing.

3. Scan your body from head to toe, noting any areas of tension or discomfort.

4. Identify what emotions you're feeling in this moment.

5. Without judgment, observe any thoughts passing through your mind.

At the end of the week, reflect on how this practice has affected your awareness of your thoughts, emotions, and behaviors.

Cognitive Restructuring

Cognitive restructuring is a technique used to identify and challenge negative thought patterns:

- **Thought Records**: Keep a log of your negative thoughts, the situations that trigger them, and the resulting emotions and behaviors.

- **Challenging Cognitive Distortions**: Learn to recognize and question common cognitive distortions like all-or-nothing thinking, overgeneralization, and catastrophizing.

- **Developing Alternative Thoughts**: Practice generating more balanced, realistic thoughts to replace negative ones.

Exercise: Thought Record

Create a thought record with the following columns:

1. Situation

2. Automatic Thought

3. Emotion and Intensity (0-100)

4. Evidence For the Thought

5. Evidence Against the Thought

6. Alternative Thought

_____

_____

_____

7. New Emotion and Intensity (0-100)

_____

_____

_____

Fill out this thought record whenever you notice a strong negative emotion or engage in toxic behavior. Over time, this practice can help you develop more balanced thinking patterns.

Emotional Regulation Techniques

Learning to regulate our emotions can help prevent toxic behaviors that often stem from emotional overwhelm:

- **Grounding Techniques**: Use your senses to connect with the present moment. For example, name five things you can see, four things you can touch, three things you can hear, two things you can smell, and one thing you can taste.

- **Progressive Muscle Relaxation**: Systematically tense and relax different muscle groups in your body to release physical tension and promote relaxation.

- **Emotion Surfing**: Instead of fighting against difficult emotions, practice observing them non-judgmentally, recognizing that they will pass like waves in the ocean.

Exercise: Creating an Emotional Regulation Toolkit

Make a list of healthy ways you can cope with intense emotions. Include activities that help you feel calm, grounded, and balanced. Your toolkit might include:

- Physical activities (e.g., going for a walk, doing yoga)

- Creative outlets (e.g., drawing, writing, playing music)

- Sensory experiences (e.g., taking a warm bath, using aromatherapy)

- Social support (e.g., calling a friend, attending a support group)

Keep this toolkit easily accessible and refer to it when you feel emotionally overwhelmed.

Self-Compassion Practice

Self-compassion involves treating ourselves with the same kindness and understanding we would offer a good friend. This can be particularly powerful in breaking the cycle of shame and self-criticism that often accompanies toxic behaviors:

- **Mindful Self-Compassion**: When you notice self-critical thoughts, pause and offer yourself words of kindness and understanding.

- **Common Humanity**: Remind yourself that everyone struggles and makes mistakes. You're not alone in your challenges.

- **Self-Compassionate Letter**: Write a letter to yourself from the perspective of a loving, compassionate friend.

Exercise: Self-Compassion Break

When you notice you're being hard on yourself, take a self-compassion break:

1. Acknowledge the difficulty of the moment: "This is really tough right now."

2. Remind yourself of our shared human experience: "Everyone struggles sometimes. I'm not alone in this."

3. Offer yourself words of kindness: "May I be kind to myself in this moment."

4. Place your hand over your heart or use another soothing touch, feeling the warmth and care you're offering yourself.

The Path Forward

Understanding the toll that toxic behaviors take on our mental health can be overwhelming, but it's an essential step in the journey toward healthier patterns. By recognizing the connections between our actions, thoughts, and emotional well-being, we open the door to positive change.

Remember, change is a process, not an event. Be patient with yourself as you work to implement these tools and strategies. Celebrate small victories, and don't be discouraged by setbacks—they're a normal part of the growth process.

In the next section, we'll explore how to translate this understanding and these coping strategies into concrete actions for changing toxic behaviors. We'll look at how to set healthy boundaries, communicate more effectively, and build more fulfilling relationships—both with others and with ourselves.

Your commitment to this process is commendable. By facing these difficult truths and working to change, you're not only improving your own life but also positively impacting everyone you interact with. Keep moving forward, one step at a time.

PART 3

ACCOUNTABILITY AND ACKNOWLEDGMENT IN OVERCOMING TOXIC BEHAVIORS

We arrive at a crucial juncture: accountability and acknowledgment. This step is often the most challenging, yet it's also the most transformative. In this section, we'll explore why accepting responsibility is essential for change, engage in exercises to acknowledge the harm caused by toxic behaviors, and examine real-life examples of how accountability leads to emotional healing.

The Crucial Role of Accepting Responsibility in Change

Accepting responsibility for our actions, especially when those actions have caused harm, can be intensely uncomfortable. It's human nature to want to avoid this discomfort, leading us to engage in various forms of denial, minimization, or blame-shifting. However, true change and growth can only occur when we fully own our behaviors and their consequences.

Why Responsibility Is Essential

- **Breaking the Cycle**: When we refuse to take responsibility, we remain trapped in patterns of toxic behavior. Accepting responsibility is the key that unlocks the door to change.

- **Empowerment**: While it may seem counterintuitive, taking responsibility is empowering. It moves us from a position of helplessness to one of agency—if we're responsible for our actions, we also have the power to change them.

- **Rebuilding Trust**: Accountability is crucial for rebuilding trust in relationships damaged by toxic behaviors. It demonstrates a commitment to change and respect for those we've hurt.

- **Self-Awareness**: The process of accepting responsibility fosters deeper self-awareness, helping us understand our triggers, motivations, and patterns of behavior.

- **Emotional Growth**: Facing our mistakes and shortcomings, while difficult, promotes emotional maturity and resilience.

The Barriers to Accountability

Understanding what holds us back from taking responsibility can help us overcome these obstacles:

- **Fear of Judgment**: We may worry that admitting our faults will lead others to think less of us.

- **Shame**: Deep-seated shame can make it feel too painful to confront our mistakes.

- **Perfectionism**: If we hold ourselves to impossible standards, admitting imperfection can feel like failure.

- **Lack of Role Models**: If we grew up in environments where accountability wasn't modeled, we may lack the skills to practice it ourselves.

- **Cognitive Dissonance**: Accepting responsibility might conflict with the image we hold of ourselves, creating psychological discomfort.

Exercise: Identifying Your Accountability Barriers

Reflect on a situation where you struggled to take responsibility for toxic behavior:

1.   What were the specific behaviors you found difficult to own?

2.   What thoughts or feelings came up when you considered taking responsibility?

3.   Which of the barriers mentioned above do you recognize in yourself?

4.   How might overcoming these barriers benefit you and your relationships?

Exercises for Acknowledging Harm Caused by Toxic Behavior

Acknowledging the harm we've caused is a critical step in the accountability process. It requires us to step out of our own perspective and truly see the impact of our actions on others. Here are some exercises to help cultivate this awareness and acknowledgment.

Exercise 1: The Impact Letter

Write a letter from the perspective of someone who has been affected by your toxic behavior. This could be a partner, friend, family member, or colleague. Try to put yourself in their shoes and articulate how your actions have impacted them emotionally, mentally, and perhaps even physically.

Guidelines for the letter:

- Be specific about the behaviors and incidents.

- Describe the immediate and long-term effects.

- Express the emotions experienced as a result of the behavior.

- Reflect on how it has affected the relationship.

- Consider the ripple effects on other aspects of their life.

After writing the letter, read it aloud to yourself. Notice any emotions or insights that arise.

The Impact Letter

Exercise 2: The Accountability Mirror

Stand in front of a mirror and have an honest conversation with yourself about your toxic behaviors. This exercise helps externalize your inner dialogue and can make the process of acknowledgment feel more concrete.

1. Look yourself in the eye and state a specific toxic behavior you've engaged in.

2. Acknowledge the harm this behavior has caused, being as specific as possible.

3. Express how this realization makes you feel.

4. State a commitment to change this behavior.

Repeat this process for different behaviors you're working on changing. It may feel uncomfortable at first, but with practice, it becomes a powerful tool for self-reflection and commitment to change.

Exercise 3: The Ripple Effect Map

Create a visual representation of how your toxic behavior affects not just the immediate target but ripples out to impact others.

1. In the center of a large piece of paper, write down a specific toxic behavior.

2. In the next ring, write the names of people directly impacted by this behavior.

3. In the outer rings, consider how these impacts might affect others - for example, if your behavior stressed your partner, how might that affect their work performance or relationships with others?

4. For each person or group affected, write down the specific impacts.

This exercise helps visualize the far-reaching consequences of our actions and can be a powerful motivator for change.

Exercise 4: The Amends List

Create a list of people you believe you've harmed through your toxic behaviors. For each person:

1. Write down the specific behaviors you're accountable for.

2. Reflect on why you engaged in these behaviors (but be careful not to use this as an excuse).

3. Consider what meaningful amends might look like for this person.

4. Decide whether making direct amends is appropriate and safe for both parties.

Remember, making amends is about taking responsibility and showing a commitment to change, not about seeking forgiveness or trying to erase the past.

Examples of How Accountability Leads to Emotional Healing

Accountability isn't just about facing the music—it's a pathway to profound emotional healing and growth. Let's explore some real-life examples of how taking responsibility can lead to positive change and restoration.

Example 1: Mary's Journey from Blame to Growth

Mary had a habit of lashing out at her partner, Brandon, whenever she felt insecure or stressed. She would criticize him harshly and then blame him for "making her" act that way. This pattern had eroded their relationship to the point where Brandon was considering leaving.

In a moment of clarity, Mary realized she needed to take responsibility for her behavior. She started by keeping a journal of her outbursts, forcing herself to acknowledge each instance without making excuses. She then took the courageous step of sitting down with Brandon and taking full responsibility for her actions, without any "buts" or attempts to shift blame.

This act of accountability was transformative. Brandon felt heard and validated, which opened the door to healing in their relationship. For Mary, owning her behavior allowed her to finally address the underlying insecurities driving it. She started therapy to work on these issues and learned healthier ways to communicate her needs.

The process wasn't easy, and there were setbacks along the way. But Mary's commitment to accountability created a foundation for lasting change. Over time, she and Brandon rebuilt trust, and Mary found she felt more secure and confident as she continued to practice responsibility and self-reflection.

Example 2: Michael's Workplace Transformation

Michael was known in his office for taking credit for others' work and throwing colleagues under the bus when projects went wrong. His behavior had created a toxic work environment, with team members reluctant to collaborate or share ideas.

The turning point came when Michael was passed over for a promotion. Instead of blaming others as he usually would, he took a hard look at his behavior. He realized that his actions, driven by insecurity and a fear of failure, were sabotaging his career and harming his colleagues.

Michael took the brave step of calling a team meeting where he openly acknowledged his toxic behaviors. He took responsibility for the negative atmosphere he had created and committed to changing. He asked for patience and feedback as he worked to improve.

Initially, his colleagues were skeptical. However, as they saw Michael making consistent efforts to change—giving credit where it was due, admitting his mistakes, and supporting team members—the office dynamic began to shift. Team morale improved, collaboration increased, and Michael found he was actually performing better without the constant energy drain of maintaining his toxic behaviors.

The process of accountability opened the door for Michael to address his underlying insecurities. He sought coaching to develop healthier leadership skills and found that the need to undermine others disappeared as he became more secure in his abilities.

Example 3: The Rodriguez Family Healing

The Rodriguez family had a generational pattern of emotional abuse, with criticism and guilt-tripping being common parenting tools. Sofia, a mother of two, recognized this pattern in her own behavior toward her children and decided it was time to break the cycle.

Sofia started by educating herself about emotional abuse and its impacts. She was horrified to realize the harm she had been causing. In a family meeting, she took full responsibility for her behavior, acknowledging specific incidents and the hurt they had caused without making any excuses.

She committed to changing her parenting approach and asked her children for their help in pointing out when she slipped into old patterns. Sofia also reached out to her own parents, sharing her realizations and setting new boundaries.

The journey wasn't smooth—undoing years of conditioning took time and effort. However, Sofia's commitment to accountability opened up new levels of communication in the family. Her children, seeing her take responsibility and make real efforts to change, began to trust her more. They felt safer expressing their feelings and needs.

Sofia's accountability also inspired reflection in her parents. While they initially became defensive, Sofia's persistence in owning her part without blaming them eventually led to deeper conversations about their family history.

Over time, the family dynamic transformed. Sofia's children learned healthy emotional expression and boundary-setting from watching her growth process. The cycle of emotional abuse was replaced with a new legacy of accountability, respect, and open communication.

Reflection: The Power of Accountability

These stories illustrate several key points about accountability:

- **It's a Process**: Accountability isn't a one-time event but an ongoing commitment to awareness and change.

- **It Inspires Trust**: When we take genuine responsibility for our actions, it opens the door for others to trust us again.

- **It Facilitates Self-Growth**: The process of being accountable often leads us to examine and address the root causes of our toxic behaviors.

- **It Has a Ripple Effect**: Our accountability can inspire change in others and shift entire relationship dynamics.

- **It's Empowering**: While facing our mistakes is uncomfortable, it ultimately empowers us to actively shape our relationships and lives.

Exercise: Your Accountability Story

Reflect on a time when you practiced genuine accountability:

1. What was the situation, and what toxic behavior did you take responsibility for?

_____

_____

_____

2. How did it feel to acknowledge your behavior and its impact?

_____

_____

3. What changes occurred in you and in your relationships as a result?

4. If you haven't had such an experience yet, imagine how taking accountability for a current issue might play out. What steps would you need to take?

The Healing Power of Accountability

As we've explored in this section, accountability and acknowledgment are not punitive measures but powerful tools for healing and growth. By accepting responsibility for our toxic behaviors, we open the door to genuine change, deeper relationships, and a more authentic way of living.

Remember that the journey of accountability is ongoing. It requires courage, humility, and a commitment to self-reflection. There are going to be uncomfortable moments and setbacks along the way. Nevertheless, with each step we take in owning our actions and their impacts, we create new possibilities for ourselves and those around us.

In the next section, we'll explore practical strategies for implementing lasting change based on this foundation of accountability. We'll look at how to translate our acknowledgments into concrete actions, set healthy boundaries, and cultivate new patterns of behavior that align with our values and support healthy relationships.

Your commitment to this accountability process is commendable. It's not an easy path, but it will lead you to profound personal growth and more fulfilling connections with others. Keep moving forward, one accountable step at a time.

PART 4

UNMASKING DARK PSYCHOLOGY AND NARCISSISM

The main condition for the achievement of love is the overcoming of one's narcissism. –Eric Fromm

Welcome to a crucial chapter in your journey toward healthier relationships and personal growth. In this chapter, we'll delve into the complex and often misunderstood realms of dark psychology and narcissism. These topics can be challenging to explore, but understanding them is vital for protecting yourself from manipulation and maintaining healthy boundaries in your relationships.

As we navigate this chapter, you may recognize behaviors in others or even in yourself. Remember, the goal is not to label or diagnose but to increase awareness and develop strategies for healthier interactions. If you find this material particularly triggering or relevant to your personal experiences, please consider seeking support from a mental health professional.

Let's begin our exploration of these darker aspects of human behavior, always keeping in mind our ultimate goal of fostering healthier, more fulfilling relationships.

Understanding Dark Psychology

Dark psychology refers to the study and application of psychological techniques used to manipulate, coerce, or influence others for personal gain or malicious purposes. While psychology as a whole aims to understand human behavior, dark psychology focuses on the more nefarious uses of this knowledge.

Recognizing Dark Psychology Tactics

Dark psychology employs various manipulation tactics. Being able to recognize these can help you protect yourself and others. Consider the following scenarios and identify which dark psychology tactic might be at play:

1. Your colleague consistently takes credit for your ideas in team meetings, but when confronted, they insist they were just "expanding on what you said."

2. A salesperson tells you that their product is almost sold out, and you need to buy now before you miss out, even though you're unsure if you really need it.

3. Your friend always seems to have a crisis whenever you have an important event or achievement to celebrate.

4. A political candidate uses vivid, emotional stories about crime to push for stricter laws, even though statistics show crime rates are actually declining.

5. Your partner frequently says things like "If you really loved me, you would..." when asking you to do something you're not comfortable with.

Reflection: For each scenario, write down which manipulation tactic you think is being used (e.g., gaslighting, scarcity principle, guilt-tripping, fear-mongering, emotional blackmail). Then, reflect on whether you've encountered similar situations in your own life. How did you respond? How might you respond differently now that you're aware of these tactics?

The Impact of Dark Psychology

While it's important to recognize dark psychology tactics, it's equally crucial to understand their impact. These manipulative techniques can have severe consequences on mental health, self-esteem, and overall well-being.

Exercise: Emotional Impact Inventory

Think about a time when you've been subjected to manipulative behavior. It could be from a personal relationship, a professional setting, or even a broader social context. Describe the situation briefly, then rate the impact it had on you in the following areas (1 being minimal impact, 10 being severe impact):

1. Self-esteem:

2. Trust in others:

3. Anxiety levels:

4. Decision-making ability:

5. Overall sense of well-being:

Looking at your ratings, which areas were most affected? How have these experiences shaped your interactions with others? What steps can you take to heal from these impacts?

_____

_____

_____

_____

Narcissism: Beyond the Myth

Narcissism is often misunderstood in popular culture. While we may casually label someone as "narcissistic" for being self-centered, true narcissism—especially when it manifests as narcissistic personality disorder (NPD)—is a complex psychological phenomenon.

The Spectrum of Narcissism

Narcissism exists on a spectrum. On one end, we have healthy self-esteem and confidence. On the other, we have pathological narcissism that can be diagnosed as NPD. Most people fall somewhere in between.

Exercise: The Narcissism Spectrum
Consider the following behaviors and traits. Place each one on a spectrum from "Healthy Self-Esteem" to "Pathological Narcissism":

- taking pride in your achievements

- needing constant admiration

- setting healthy boundaries

- lacking empathy for others

- being confident in your abilities

- feeling entitled to special treatment

- being able to laugh at yourself

- having an exaggerated sense of self-importance

- appreciating compliments

- exploiting others for personal gain

Where did you place each trait? Were some difficult to categorize? How might this spectrum help you differentiate between healthy confidence and problematic narcissism in your own life and relationships?

_____

_____

_____

_____

_____

Types of Narcissism

Narcissism can manifest in different ways. The three primary types are:

- **Grandiose Narcissism**: Characterized by overt expressions of superiority and entitlement

- **Vulnerable Narcissism**: Marked by hypersensitivity to criticism and social withdrawal

- **Malignant Narcissism**: The most severe form, combining narcissism with antisocial features

Exercise: Identifying Narcissistic Behaviors

For each type of narcissism, write down three behaviors or traits that might be associated with it. Then, reflect on whether you've encountered these behaviors in your personal or professional life. How did you handle these situations? What might you do differently with your current understanding?

- **Grandiose Narcissism:**

- **Vulnerable Narcissism:**

- **Malignant Narcissism:**

The Narcissistic Relationship Cycle

Relationships with narcissists often follow a predictable pattern: idealization, devaluation, and discard. Understanding this cycle can help you recognize and navigate narcissistic relationships.

Exercise: Mapping the Narcissistic Relationship Cycle

Think about a relationship you've had (or someone close to you has had) that you suspect might have been with a narcissist. Try to map out the stages of the relationship:

1. **Idealization**: How did the relationship begin? What made it feel special or intense?

---

2. **Devaluation**: When did things start to change? What behaviors signaled this shift?

3. **Discard**: How did the relationship end (or how is it continuing in a cycle of devaluation and intermittent reinforcement)?

What patterns do you notice? Were there any red flags in the idealization stage that you can now recognize? How might you protect yourself from this cycle in future relationships?

Protecting Yourself from Dark Psychology and Narcissism

Now that we've explored dark psychology and narcissism, let's focus on strategies to protect yourself from these harmful dynamics.

Setting and Maintaining Boundaries

Boundaries are crucial in any relationship, but they're especially important when dealing with manipulative or narcissistic individuals.

Exercise: Boundary Setting

List three important boundaries you need in your relationships. For each boundary, write:

1. What the boundary is

_____

_____

_____

2. Why it's important to you

_____

_____

_____

3. How you'll communicate this boundary to others

4. What consequences you'll enforce if the boundary is violated

How does it feel to articulate these boundaries? What challenges do you anticipate in maintaining them? How might strong boundaries protect you from manipulation and narcissistic abuse?

Developing a Strong Sense of Self

A strong sense of self is your best defense against manipulation and narcissistic abuse.

Exercise: Core Values Identification

List your top five core values. For each value, write:

1. Why this value is important to you

2. A time when you honored this value, even when it was difficult

3. How this value guides your decisions and actions

How can staying connected to your core values help you resist manipulation? How might these values serve as a compass when you're dealing with difficult people or situations?

Healing and Moving Forward

If you've been affected by dark psychology or narcissistic abuse, healing is possible. While the journey can be challenging, understanding what you've experienced is a crucial first step.

Exercise: Letter to Your Future Self
Write a letter to your future self, one who has healed from these experiences. Include:

- acknowledgment of what you've been through

- the strengths you've discovered in yourself through this process

- the boundaries you're committed to maintaining

- your hopes for future relationships

Seal this letter and set a date for opening it in the future. This exercise can serve as both a commitment to your healing journey and a touchstone to return to when you need encouragement.

Letter to Your Future Self

Chapter Takeaways

Understanding dark psychology and narcissism is a powerful step in protecting yourself from manipulation and cultivating healthier relationships. Remember, if you recognize these patterns in your significant relationships, it's important to seek support from a qualified mental health professional.

As we move forward, we'll build on this knowledge to explore healing from toxic relationships and building healthy, fulfilling connections. Keep in mind that your journey is unique, and it's okay to move at your own pace. Every step you take toward understanding and setting boundaries is a step toward a healthier, more authentic life.

- Dark psychology involves manipulative tactics used for personal gain or malicious purposes.

- Narcissism exists on a spectrum, with pathological narcissism at the extreme end.

- Recognizing the narcissistic relationship cycle can help you avoid or exit harmful relationships.

- Setting and maintaining strong boundaries is crucial for protecting yourself from manipulation and abuse.

- Developing a strong sense of self, grounded in your core values, is your best defense against dark psychology and narcissism.

- Healing from narcissistic abuse or manipulation is possible, and seeking professional help can be a valuable part of this journey.

SECTION 3

ACCOUNTABILITY - BUILDING LASTING CHANGE

As we enter the final phase of our journey toward overcoming toxic behaviors and building healthier relationships, we arrive at a crucial juncture: transforming our newfound awareness and skills into lasting change. This section, "Accountability—Building Lasting Change," will equip you with the strategies and mindset necessary to sustain your progress and continue growing long after you've finished this book.

The path to lasting change is rarely smooth or linear. It requires dedication, resilience, and, most importantly, accountability. Accountability is the thread that weaves together your intentions, actions, and long-term success. It's the commitment you make not just to others but to yourself to follow through on your goals and aspirations. Without accountability, even the best intentions can falter in the face of old habits and unexpected challenges.

In the following three chapters, we'll explore different facets of accountability and how they contribute to building lasting change:

Creating a Support System for Accountability: Here, we'll delve into the power of community in sustaining personal growth. You'll learn how to choose and work with an accountability partner, leverage group support for major life changes, and make your commitment to change public in a way that feels authentic and motivating. Remember, while the journey of change is personal, you don't have to walk it alone.

Handling Setbacks and Relapse: Change is rarely a straight path forward, and setbacks are a normal part of the process. In this chapter, we'll equip you with strategies to identify triggers before they lead to relapse, create a structured plan for bouncing back from setbacks, and, most importantly, approach these challenges with self-compassion and a growth mindset. You'll learn how to turn moments of difficulty into opportunities for deeper learning and stronger resolve.

Sustaining Long-Term Accountability: The final chapter focuses on integrating accountability into your daily life for the long haul. We'll explore how to develop a consistent personal check-in routine, maintain productive accountability conversations with partners or groups, and build accountability practices into future relationships. These strategies will help you maintain momentum and continue growing even as your initial motivation may wax and wane.

As we start this final section, it's important to acknowledge the significant progress you've already made. The fact that you're here, ready to tackle the challenge of lasting change, is a testament to your commitment and growth. At the same time, it's natural to feel some apprehension about the road ahead. Lasting change requires us to step out of our comfort zones, challenge deeply ingrained habits, and sometimes, reimagine our very identities.

Remember, the goal isn't perfection but progress. Each step you take toward accountability and lasting change is a victory, no matter how small it may seem. The skills and mindsets you'll develop in these chapters are not just about overcoming toxic behaviors—they're life skills that will serve you in all areas of personal growth and relationship building.

As we dive into these final chapters, I encourage you to approach them with an open mind and a willingness to experiment. Not every strategy will resonate with everyone, and that's okay. The key is finding the best accountability tools and practices for you and your unique situation.

You've already demonstrated tremendous courage and self-awareness by coming this far. Now, let's take that final step together—from understanding and intention to lasting, meaningful change. Your journey toward healthier behaviors and relationships doesn't end with this book; in many ways, it's just beginning. But with the accountability strategies you'll learn in these chapters, you'll be well-equipped to continue growing, learning, and thriving long after you turn the last page.

Let's begin this final, transformative phase of our journey together.

PART 1

CREATING A SUPPORT SYSTEM FOR ACCOUNTABILITY

As we continue on the journey of overcoming toxic behaviors and building lasting change, one of the most powerful tools at our disposal is a strong support system. In this chapter, we'll explore how to create and maintain a network of support that will help you stay accountable, motivated, and on track with your personal growth goals.

We'll dive into three key aspects of building your support system: choosing an accountability partner, leveraging group accountability, and making your commitment public. Each of these strategies offers unique benefits and challenges, and by the end of this chapter, you'll have a comprehensive toolkit for creating a support system tailored to your needs.

Remember, seeking support is not a sign of weakness but a testament to your commitment to change. Let's begin this crucial step in your journey toward lasting transformation.

Choosing an Accountability Partner

Choosing to go on a journey of personal change can be daunting, and having a dedicated ally can make all the difference. An accountability partner is that ally—someone who walks alongside you, offering support, honest feedback, and motivation. In this section, we'll explore why having an accountability partner is crucial for sustained change, how to select the right person for this important role, and guidelines for making the most of this partnership. By the end of this section, you'll be equipped to find and nurture a powerful accountability relationship that can significantly boost your chances of success in overcoming toxic behaviors.

Why Accountability Partners are Essential for Sustained Change

An accountability partner is more than just a cheerleader; they're a crucial ally in your journey of personal growth. Here's why having an accountability partner is so important:

- **Consistent Support**: Unlike sporadic encouragement from friends or family, an accountability partner provides regular, focused support.

- **Objective Perspective**: They can offer an outside view of your progress and challenges, helping you see blind spots you might miss.

- **Motivation Boost**: Knowing someone is checking in on your progress can be a powerful motivator to stick to your commitments.

- **Shared Learning**: As you both work on personal growth, you can learn from each other's experiences and insights.

- **Celebration of Milestones**: An accountability partner helps acknowledge and celebrate your progress, boosting your motivation.

How to Select the Right Person to Support Your Journey

Choosing the right accountability partner is crucial for the success of this relationship. Consider these factors:

- **Shared Goals**: While they don't need to be working on the exact same issues, it helps if your partner has similar personal growth aspirations.

- **Reliability**: Choose someone who is dependable and will consistently show up for check-ins.

- **Honesty**: Your partner should be able to give you truthful feedback, even when it's difficult.

- **Empathy**: Look for someone who can balance honesty with understanding and support.

- **Availability**: Ensure your schedules align enough for regular check-ins.

- **Mutual Benefit**: The relationship should be reciprocal, with both parties supporting each other.

Exercise: Potential Accountability Partner Assessment

Make a list of potential accountability partners. For each person, rate them on a scale of 1-5 (1 being low, 5 being high) in each of the above categories. The person with the highest total score might be your best choice.

Guidelines for Regular Check-Ins and Progress Discussions

Once you've chosen your accountability partner, establish clear guidelines for your partnership:

1. **Set a Regular Schedule**: Decide on the frequency of check-ins (weekly is often a good start) and stick to it.

2. **Define the Format**: Will you meet in person, over video call, or through text? Choose a method that works for both of you.

3. **Establish a Structure**: Create a template for your check-ins. For example:

o Share wins from the past week.

o Discuss challenges faced.

o Review progress on goals.

o Set intentions for the coming week.

4. **Practice Active Listening**: When your partner is sharing, focus on understanding rather than immediately offering solutions.

5. **Offer Constructive Feedback**: Frame feedback positively and specifically.

6. **Celebrate Progress**: Acknowledge and celebrate each other's achievements, no matter how small.

7. **Respect Boundaries**: Establish what level of "tough love" is acceptable and respect each other's limits.

8. **Regularly Review**: Periodically assess how the partnership is working and be open to adjusting your approach.

Exercise: Accountability Partnership Agreement

Draft an agreement with your chosen accountability partner covering the points above. Having this in writing can help clarify expectations and commitments for both parties.

Accountability Partnership Agreement

Group Accountability for Major Life Changes

While one-on-one accountability partnerships offer personalized support, there's a unique power in group dynamics when it comes to major life changes. A support group can provide a diverse range of perspectives, shared experiences, and a sense of community that can be incredibly motivating. In this section, we'll delve into the benefits of group support for personal growth, explore how to find or form a support group specifically focused on overcoming toxic behaviors, and provide tips for both leading and participating effectively in group discussions. Whether you're joining an existing group or starting your own, you'll learn how to harness the collective energy of a group to propel your personal growth journey forward.

The Benefits of Group Support for Personal Growth

While one-on-one accountability partnerships are powerful, group support offers unique advantages:

- **Diverse Perspectives**: A group provides a range of viewpoints and experiences to learn from.

- **Increased Motivation**: Seeing others succeed can inspire and motivate you in your own journey.

- **Shared Resources**: Group members can share tools, techniques, and resources they've found helpful.

- **Reduced Isolation**: Knowing others are facing similar challenges can reduce feelings of loneliness or shame.

- **Opportunity for Leadership**: As you progress, you may have opportunities to mentor or support newer group members.

How to Find or Form a Support Group for Overcoming Toxic Behaviors

1. **Look for Existing Groups:**

   o   Check local community centers, libraries, or religious organizations.

   o   Search online platforms like Meetup.com or Facebook groups.

   o   Inquire at mental health clinics or counseling centers.

2. **Form Your Own Group:**

   o   Reach out to friends or acquaintances who might be interested.

   o   Post about your intention to start a group on social media or local community boards.

   o   Consider partnering with a mental health professional to co-facilitate.

3. **Decide on Group Structure:**

   o   Will it be in-person, online, or a hybrid?

   o   How often will you meet?

   o   What will be the format of meetings?

4. **Establish Group Guidelines:**

   o   confidentiality rules

   o   respectful communication expectations

   o   commitment requirements

Exercise: Group Vision Board

If you're starting a group, create a vision board (physical or digital) that represents the group's goals and values. This can serve as a powerful visual reminder of your shared commitment to growth.

Tips for Leading or Participating in Group Discussions

For Group Leaders:

1. **Prepare an Agenda**: Have a clear structure for each meeting.

2. **Encourage Participation**: Ensure everyone has a chance to share.

3. **Manage Time**: Keep discussions on track and balanced.

4. **Foster a Safe Environment**: Reinforce confidentiality and respect.

5. **Provide Resources**: Share relevant articles, exercises, or tools.

For Participants:

1. **Be Present**: Engage fully in discussions and activities.

2. **Practice Active Listening**: Focus on understanding others without judgment.

3. **Share Honestly**: Be open about your challenges and successes.

4. **Offer Support**: Encourage and support other group members.

5. **Follow Through**: Complete any "homework" or commitments made to the group.

Exercise: Personal Participation Plan

Create a personal plan for how you'll engage in group meetings. Include:

- how you'll prepare for each meeting

- your commitment to participation (e.g., sharing at least one challenge and one success each meeting)

- how you'll apply insights gained from the group in your daily life

Personal Participation Plan

_____

_____

_____

_____

_____

_____

_____

_____

Making Your Commitment Public

In our increasingly connected world, public declarations of intent can be a powerful tool for accountability. Sharing your commitment to change with a wider audience - whether it's your social media followers, your broader circle of friends, or an online community - can add an extra layer of motivation and support to your journey.

However, it's important to approach public accountability thoughtfully and responsibly. In this section, we'll explore how publicly declaring your goals can enhance your accountability, discuss the role that social media and friends can play in supporting your journey, and provide guidelines for using online platforms effectively and responsibly for public accountability. By the end of this section, you'll have strategies for leveraging public commitment in a way that supports your growth while maintaining healthy boundaries.

How Publicly Declaring Your Goals Adds Accountability

Making your commitment to change public can significantly boost your accountability:

- **Increased Motivation**: Knowing others are aware of your goals can push you to stay committed.

- **External Encouragement**: Public commitments often lead to support and encouragement from others.

- **Clarity and Commitment**: Articulating your goals publicly requires clarity, reinforcing your own commitment.

- **Social Pressure**: While not always comfortable, social pressure can be a powerful motivator.

- **Inspiration to Others**: Your public commitment might inspire others to make positive changes in their lives.

The Role of Social Media and Friends in Holding You Accountable

Social media and friends can play a significant role in your accountability journey:

- **Progress Updates**: Regular posts about your progress can keep you on track.

- **Support Network**: Friends can offer encouragement, advice, and support.

- **Milestone Celebrations**: Sharing achievements, even small ones, can boost motivation.

- **Resource Sharing**: Friends might share helpful resources or connect you with others on similar journeys.

- **Reality Checks**: Close friends who know your goals can provide gentle reminders if they notice you slipping.

Exercise: Crafting Your Public Commitment Statement

Write a clear, concise statement of your commitment to change. Include:

- the specific behaviors you're working to change

- why this change is important to you

- how you plan to achieve your goals

- how others can support you

Using Online Platforms Responsibly for Public Accountability

While public accountability can be powerful, it's important to use online platforms responsibly:

- **Choose Your Platforms Wisely**: Select platforms where you feel comfortable sharing and have a supportive network.

- **Set Boundaries**: Decide in advance what you're comfortable sharing and what you'll keep private.

- **Be Honest but Positive**: Share both successes and challenges, but frame challenges as opportunities for growth.

- **Protect Your Privacy**: Be cautious about sharing extremely personal details or information that could be used harmfully.

- **Engage Meaningfully**: Respond to comments and engage with others on similar journeys.

- **Stay Consistent**: Regular updates are more effective than sporadic, intense bursts of sharing.

- **Use Accountability Apps**: Consider using apps designed for habit tracking and public accountability.

- **Create a Hashtag**: A personal hashtag can help you and others track your journey.

Exercise: Social Media Accountability Plan

Create a plan for using social media as an accountability tool:

- Which platforms will you use?

- How often will you post updates?

- What type of content will you share?

- How will you engage with supporters?

- What boundaries will you set to protect your privacy and mental health?

Chapter Takeaways

Creating a robust support system is a crucial step in your journey toward overcoming toxic behaviors and building lasting change. Whether through one-on-one partnerships, group support, or public commitments, surrounding yourself with accountability can significantly boost your chances of success.

Remember, the goal is to create a support system that works for you. Finding the right balance may take some trial and error, and that's okay. Be patient with yourself, and don't be afraid to adjust your approach as you learn what works best for you.

As you move forward, keep in mind that accountability is a two-way street. Just as you receive support, be prepared to offer it to others. This reciprocal relationship helps others and can deepen your commitment to change.

Your commitment to change is commendable. By creating a strong support system, you're setting yourself up for success. Keep moving forward, one step at a time, with your accountability partners by your side.

PART 2

HANDLING SETBACKS AND RELAPSE

In the journey of overcoming toxic behaviors and building lasting change, setbacks and relapses are not just possible—they're often a natural part of the process. While they can feel discouraging, these moments offer valuable opportunities for learning and growth. This section will equip you with strategies to identify potential triggers, create a robust relapse recovery plan, and bounce back stronger after experiencing a setback. Remember, the path to change is rarely linear, and how we respond to challenges often defines our ultimate success.

Identifying Triggers Before They Cause Relapse

Recognizing and managing triggers is a crucial skill in preventing relapses. Triggers are situations, emotions, or environments that can prompt a return to toxic behaviors. By learning to identify these triggers early, we can take proactive steps to manage them effectively, significantly reducing the risk of relapse.

Recognizing Emotional or Environmental Triggers Early

Triggers can be broadly categorized into emotional and environmental factors:

- **Emotional Triggers:**

  o stress

  o anger

  o loneliness

  o boredom

  o anxiety

  o disappointment

- **Environmental Triggers:**

  o certain locations

  o specific people or relationships

  o time of day or year

  o work situations

  o social events

Let's engage in a trigger mapping exercise to help you identify and understand your personal triggers.

Exercise: Trigger Mapping

Objective: Create a personal trigger map to identify and understand your emotional and environmental triggers.

Materials needed: Paper and pen, a digital document or you can do it down below.

Instructions:

1. Draw two columns on your paper, labeling them "Emotional Triggers" and "Environmental Triggers."

2. Under each column, list potential triggers. Aim for at least 5 in each category.

3. Next to each trigger, rate its intensity on a scale of 1-10 (1 being mild, 10 being severe).

4. For each trigger, write down one or two early warning signs that indicate this trigger is present.

5. Look for patterns or connections between triggers. Draw lines connecting related triggers.

Emotional Triggers	Rate	Warning Signs	Environmental Triggers	Rate	Warning Signs

Reflection:

- What are your three most intense triggers?

- Do you notice any patterns in your triggers?

- Which triggers might be easiest to address first?

How to Proactively Deal With Triggers Before Relapse Happens

Once you've identified your triggers, developing strategies to manage them is key:

- **Mindfulness Practices**: Regular mindfulness meditation can increase your awareness of triggers as they arise.

- **Stress Management Techniques**: Develop a toolkit of stress-reduction strategies like deep breathing, progressive muscle relaxation, or guided imagery.

- **Lifestyle Adjustments**: Consider changes to your routine or environment that can reduce exposure to triggers.

- **Building a Support Network**: Identify people you can reach out to when you feel triggered.

- **Healthy Coping Mechanisms**: Develop alternative behaviors to replace toxic ones when triggered.

Now, let's create a specific plan for managing your most significant triggers.

Exercise: Trigger Response Plan
Objective: Develop specific strategies to manage your high-intensity triggers.

Materials needed: Your completed trigger map, paper and pen, or a digital document.

Instructions:

1. Select the three triggers you rated highest in intensity from your trigger map.

2. For each of these triggers, complete the following table:

3. In the "Coping Strategy" columns, list three healthy ways you can respond when this trigger arises.

4. In the "Support Person" column, write the name of someone you can contact for support.

5. In the "Positive Affirmation" column, write a short, encouraging statement to remind yourself of your commitment to change.

Trigger	Coping Strategy 1	Coping Strategy 2	Coping Strategy 3	Support Person	Positive Affirmation

Reflection:

- How confident do you feel about implementing these strategies?

- Are there any additional resources or skills you need to acquire to better manage these triggers?

Case Studies of Relapse Prevention

To illustrate how these strategies can work in real-life situations, let's look at two case studies:

Case Study 1: Jill's Workplace Stress

Jill identified workplace stress as a major trigger for her passive-aggressive behavior. She developed a three-step plan:

1. Five-minute meditation breaks during the workday

2. Weekly check-ins with her accountability partner

3. Assertiveness training to better communicate her needs at work

Result: Jill reported a 70% reduction in workplace-triggered incidents over three months.

Case Study 2: Michael's Social Anxiety

Michael recognized that large social gatherings often triggered his manipulative behaviors. His prevention strategy included:

1. Gradual exposure therapy, starting with small gatherings

2. Pre-event positive visualization exercises

3. Setting a time limit for events and having an exit strategy

Result: Michael successfully navigated three large events without relapse, reporting increased comfort and confidence.

Building a Relapse Recovery Plan

While prevention is ideal, having a structured plan for dealing with setbacks is equally important. A well-crafted relapse recovery plan can turn a potential crisis into an opportunity for growth and learning.

How to Create a Structured Plan for Dealing With Setbacks

Let's create a personal relapse recovery plan that you can rely on when facing challenges.

Exercise: Personal Relapse Recovery Plan
Objective: Create a structured plan for dealing with setbacks or relapses.

Materials needed: Paper and pen or a digital document

Instructions:

1. Create a table with five rows labeled: Immediate Response, Reach Out, Self-Care, Reflect and Learn, Adjust and Recommit.

2. For each row, fill in specific actions you will take:

3. Under "Immediate Response," include actions like stopping the behavior, removing yourself from the situation, or using a grounding technique.

4. For "Reach Out," list specific people or resources you can contact.

5. In "Self-Care," include nurturing activities that don't involve toxic behaviors.

6. Under "Reflect and Learn," write down questions you'll ask yourself to understand what led to the setback.

7. For "Adjust and Recommit," include ways you'll update your prevention strategies and renew your commitment.

Immediate Response	
Reach Out	
Self-Care	
Reflect and Learn	
Adjust and Recommit	

Reflection:

- How does having this plan make you feel about facing potential setbacks?

- Are there any areas of this plan you'd like to strengthen further?

Reflection Exercises to Understand What Led to Relapse

When a setback occurs, it's crucial to reflect on the experience to gain insights and strengthen your prevention strategies. Here are some questions to guide your reflection:

1. **Situation Analysis**

   o What was happening just before the relapse?

o   What thoughts and feelings were you experiencing?

_____

_____

_____

2. Trigger Identification

o   Were there any new or unexpected triggers?

_____

_____

_____

o   How did familiar triggers manifest differently this time?

_____

_____

_____

3. Response Evaluation

o   How did you initially respond to the trigger?

_____

_____

_____

o   At what point did you realize you were at risk of relapse?

4. Support System Review

o   Did you reach out for support? Why or why not?

o   How could your support system be strengthened?

5. Learning Extraction

o   What's the most important lesson from this experience?

o   How can you apply this lesson to strengthen your recovery?

Real-World Examples of How Setbacks Can Strengthen Your Journey

Example 1: Alex's Communication Breakthrough

After relapsing into passive-aggressive behavior during a family conflict, Alex realized he had never learned to express anger healthily. This insight led him to:

1.   Enroll in an anger management course

2.   Practice "I feel" statements with his therapist

3.   Establish a "cool down" routine for heated moments

Result: Alex reported that this setback ultimately improved his relationship with his family, as he learned to communicate more directly and effectively.

Example 2: Emma's Self-Awareness Leap

Emma's relapse into manipulative behavior in her romantic relationship revealed a deep-seated fear of abandonment. This realization prompted her to:

1.   Start trauma-focused therapy to address childhood experiences

2.   Practice vulnerability exercises with her partner

3.   Develop a self-soothing routine for moments of insecurity

Result: Emma's relationship strengthened as she became more self-aware and developed healthier attachment patterns.

Bouncing Back After Relapse

Experiencing a relapse can be disheartening, but it's how we respond to these setbacks that truly defines our journey. With the right mindset and tools, we can use these experiences as springboards for growth and renewed commitment.

The Importance of Self-Compassion When Relapses Happen

Self-compassion is crucial in the aftermath of a relapse. It involves treating yourself with the same kindness and understanding you would offer a good friend. Here's why it's so important:

- **Reduces Shame**: Self-compassion counteracts the shame that often accompanies relapse, which can lead to a destructive cycle.

- **Promotes Learning**: A compassionate approach allows you to view the relapse objectively and learn from it.

- **Maintains Motivation**: Self-compassion helps you stay motivated to continue your journey rather than giving up in discouragement.

- **Builds Resilience**: Practicing self-compassion during difficult times builds emotional resilience for future challenges.

Let's practice self-compassion with the following exercise:

Exercise: Self-Compassion Letter

Objective: Practice self-compassion in the face of setbacks.

Materials needed: Paper and pen, a digital document or do it down below.

Instructions:

1. Imagine that a close friend has experienced the same setback or relapse that you have.

2. Write a letter to yourself from the perspective of this kind, compassionate friend.

3. In your letter, include the following elements:

4. Acknowledge the difficulty of the situation.

5. Express understanding and acceptance.

6. Offer words of comfort and encouragement.

7. Remind yourself of your strengths and past successes.

8. Express confidence in your ability to move forward and grow.

9. After writing the letter, set it aside for a few hours or a day.

10. Come back and read the letter to yourself, allowing yourself to feel the compassion and support.

Self-Compassion Letter

Reflection:

- How did it feel to write this letter?

- How did it feel to read it later?

- What was the most impactful part of this exercise for you?

How to Use Setbacks as Learning Opportunities

- **Conduct a Non-Judgmental Review**

  o Examine the circumstances of the relapse without blame or criticism.

  o Look for patterns or new insights about your triggers and behaviors.

- **Identify Skill Gaps**

  o Did the relapse reveal any areas where you need to develop new coping skills?

  o Are there resources or support systems you could add to your recovery toolkit?

- **Refine Your Strategies**

  o Based on what you've learned, how can you adjust your prevention plan?

  o Are there early warning signs you can now recognize and address earlier?

- **Set New Goals**

  o Use the insights gained to set specific, achievable goals for moving forward.

  o Consider how these goals align with your overall vision for change.

- **Share and Seek Feedback**

  o Discuss your learnings with your support system.

  o Be open to their insights and suggestions for your path forward.

Exercises to Rebuild Confidence After a Relapse

Rebuilding confidence after a setback is crucial for moving forward. Here's a structured plan to help you regain your footing:

Exercise: Confidence-Building Action Plan

Objective: Create a structured plan to rebuild confidence after a setback.

Materials needed: Paper and pen or a digital document

Instructions:

1. Create a weekly plan that incorporates elements from the confidence-building exercises mentioned earlier.

2. Use the following table as a template:

	Activity	Time Allocated	Notes
Sunday			
Monday			
Tuesday			
Wednesday			
Thursday			
Friday			
Saturday			

Customize the activities and time allocations to fit your schedule and needs. Commit to following this plan for at least four weeks.

Reflection:

- After each week, review your progress:

o Which activities were most helpful?

_____

_____

o What challenges did you face in sticking to the plan?

_____

_____

o How has your confidence changed over the week?

_____

_____

- Adjust your plan as needed based on your reflections.

Chapter Takeaways

Setbacks and relapses, while challenging, are not the end of your journey—they're part of it. By learning to identify triggers, creating a robust relapse recovery plan, and approaching setbacks with self-compassion and a growth mindset, you can turn these experiences into powerful catalysts for lasting change.

Remember, every step forward, even if it comes after a step back, is progress. Your commitment to this process, even in the face of challenges, is commendable. As you continue on your path, carry with you the knowledge that setbacks don't define you—your resilience and determination to grow do.

PART 3

SUSTAINING LONG -TERM ACCOUNTABILITY

As we progress in our journey of overcoming toxic behaviors and building healthier relationships, the challenge shifts from initial change to long-term sustainability. Sustaining accountability over time is crucial for cementing new habits and ensuring lasting transformation. This section will equip you with strategies and tools for maintaining accountability to yourself and others, creating a supportive structure for ongoing growth and self-reflection.

We'll explore how to develop a personal accountability routine, leverage partner check-ins for mutual support, and integrate accountability practices into future relationships. By the end of this section, you'll have a robust toolkit for sustaining your commitment to change and continual personal growth.

Developing a Weekly Accountability Check-In Routine

Establishing a regular personal check-in routine is fundamental to sustaining long-term accountability. This practice helps you stay connected with your goals, track your progress, and identify areas for improvement consistently.

How to Schedule Regular Personal Check-Ins

1. **Choose a Consistent Time**: Select a day and time each week when you're likely to have privacy and mental space for reflection. Many find Sunday evenings or Monday mornings effective for weekly reviews.

2. **Set a Calendar Reminder**: Use your digital calendar or phone to set a recurring reminder for your check-in time.

3. **Create a Conducive Environment**: Choose a quiet, comfortable space for your check-ins. This could be a cozy corner at home or a peaceful spot in nature.

4. **Prepare Your Materials**: Have your journal, any tracking tools, and this guide readily available for your check-in sessions.

5. **Start Small and Build**: Begin with 15-20 minute sessions and gradually increase the duration as you become more comfortable with the process.

Exercise: Designing Your Weekly Check-In Routine
Objective: Create a personalized weekly check-in plan.

Materials needed: Calendar, paper and pen, or digital planning tool

Instructions:

1. Identify your ideal check-in day and time.

2. List 3-5 elements you want to include in your check-in (e.g., goal review, emotional health assessment, relationship reflection).

3. Allocate time for each element.

4. Describe your ideal check-in environment.

5. Set up calendar reminders for the next month of check-ins.

177

Reflection:

- What potential obstacles might interfere with your check-in routine?

_____

_____

_____

- How can you proactively address these obstacles?

_____

_____

_____

Tools for Assessing Emotional and Relational Health Weekly

Regular assessment of your emotional and relational health is crucial for tracking progress and identifying areas that need attention. Here are some effective tools:

- **Emotion Tracking**: Use a mood tracker app or a simple chart to record your daily emotional states. Look for patterns over time.

- **Relationship Satisfaction Scale**: Rate your satisfaction in key relationships on a scale of 1-10 each week. Note any significant changes or trends.

- **Behavior Frequency Log**: Track the frequency of both positive behaviors you're trying to increase and negative behaviors you're working to reduce.

- **Stress Level Assessment**: Use a 1-10 scale to rate your overall stress level for the week. Identify major stressors and your responses to them.

- **Gratitude Practice**: List three things you're grateful for each day. Review these at your weekly check-in to boost positivity and perspective.

- **Goal Progress Tracker**: Create a visual representation (like a progress bar) for each of your major goals. Update it weekly to see your advancement.

Exercise: Creating Your Weekly Health Assessment Toolkit

Objective: Develop a personalized set of tools for assessing your emotional and relational health.

Materials needed: Paper and pen or digital document

Instructions:

1. Review the tools mentioned above and select 3-4 that resonate with you.

2. For each selected tool, create a template or find an app that you can use consistently.

3. Design a weekly assessment form that incorporates your chosen tools. Here's a sample structure:

Date	Mood Rating(1-10)	Top 3 Emotions	Relationship Satisfaction (1-10)	Stress Level(1-10)	Gratitude List	Goal Progress

Commit to filling out this form during each weekly check-in for at least one month.

Reflection:

- After using these tools for a month, which did you find most insightful?

- How might you adjust your toolkit to make it more effective or easier to use consistently?

Keeping a Reflection Journal to Document Progress

A reflection journal is a powerful tool for documenting your journey, gaining insights, and tracking your growth over time. Here's how to make the most of this practice:

1. **Choose Your Medium**: Decide whether you prefer writing in a physical journal or using a digital platform. Choose what feels most comfortable and accessible for you.

2. **Set a Structure**: While free-form writing can be beneficial, having some structure can help guide your reflections. Consider using prompts or sections to organize your thoughts.

3. **Be Consistent**: Aim to write in your journal at least weekly, ideally during your check-in sessions. Even brief entries are valuable if they're consistent.

4. **Be Honest**: Your journal is a private space for self-reflection. Be truthful about your experiences, thoughts, and feelings.

5. **Review Regularly**: Periodically review past entries to observe patterns, progress, and areas for growth.

Exercise: Structuring Your Reflection Journal
Objective: Create a template for your weekly reflection journal entries.

Materials needed: Journal or digital document

Instructions:

1. Design a template for your weekly entries that includes the following sections:

o Week Overview: Brief summary of key events or experiences

o Emotional Landscape: Reflection on your emotional states during the week

o Relationship Insights: Observations about your interactions and relationships

o Progress and Challenges: Notes on advancements toward your goals and any setbacks

o Learnings and Insights: Key takeaways or realizations from the week

o Next Week's Intentions: Goals or focus areas for the coming week

2. Write your first entry using this template.

3. At the end of your entry, reflect on the following:

o How did using this template feel?

o What insights did you gain that you might have missed without this structured reflection?

o How might you adjust the template to better suit your needs?

Reflection:

- After using this journal structure for a few weeks, how has it impacted your self-awareness and accountability?

- In what ways could you deepen your journaling practice to support your growth further?

Partner Accountability Check-Ins

While self-reflection is crucial, partnering with someone else for accountability can significantly enhance your growth journey. A supportive accountability partner can offer perspective, encouragement, and constructive feedback.

How to Maintain Regular Accountability Conversations

1. **Choose the Right Partner**: Select someone who is also committed to personal growth and who you trust to be honest and supportive.

2. **Set Clear Expectations**: Discuss and agree on the frequency, duration, and format of your check-ins.

3. **Create a Structure**: Develop a basic agenda for your conversations to ensure they're productive and focused.

4. **Be Prepared**: Before each check-in, reflect on your progress, challenges, and goals so you can share meaningfully.

5. **Practice Active Listening**: When your partner is sharing, focus on understanding their perspective fully before responding.

6. **Offer Constructive Feedback**: Frame your observations and suggestions in a supportive, growth-oriented manner.

7. **Celebrate Successes**: Acknowledge and celebrate each other's progress, no matter how small.

8. **Adjust as Needed**: Regularly evaluate the effectiveness of your check-ins and be willing to adjust your approach.

Scripts for Constructive Conversations About Progress

Having a framework for your conversations can help ensure they're both supportive and productive. Here are some script templates you can adapt:

1. **Opening the Conversation**: "I'm looking forward to catching up on our progress. Shall we start by sharing our biggest win from the past week?"

2. **Discussing Challenges**: "What's been your most significant challenge lately? How have you been approaching it?"

3. **Offering Feedback**: "I've noticed [specific observation]. How do you feel about that? Would you like to hear my perspective on it?"

4. **Providing Encouragement**: "I'm really impressed by how you handled [specific situation]. That shows real growth in [relevant area]."

5. **Addressing Setbacks**: "It sounds like you've had a setback with [specific issue]. That must be frustrating. What do you think you can learn from this experience?"

6. **Setting Goals**: "What's one specific goal you'd like to focus on this coming week? How can I support you in achieving it?"

7. **Closing the Conversation**: "Thank you for sharing so openly. Is there anything else you'd like to discuss before we wrap up?"

Exercise: Crafting Your Accountability Conversation Guide
Objective: Create a personalized guide for your accountability conversations.

Materials needed: Paper and pen or digital document, or do it down below.

Instructions:

1. Review the script templates above and select 3-4 that resonate with you.

2. Adapt these scripts to fit your personal style and the specific goals you're working on.

3. Create a conversation flow that includes:

o   a warm opening

o   progress review

o   challenge discussion

o   goal setting for the coming week

o   supportive closing

4. Write out your adapted scripts and conversation flow.

5. Practice delivering these scripts aloud to become comfortable with them.

Reflection:

- How does having this conversation guide make you feel about your upcoming accountability check-ins?

- In what ways might you need to adjust your language or approach to best support your accountability partner?

Scheduling Regular Accountability "Dates" for Relationship Health

Treating your accountability check-ins as important "dates" can help prioritize these conversations and make them more enjoyable. Here's how to approach this:

1. **Set a Regular Schedule**: Choose a consistent day and time for your check-ins. This regularity helps build the habit and ensures consistent support.

2. **Create a Positive Atmosphere**: If meeting in person, choose a pleasant location like a quiet café or park. For virtual meetings, ensure you have a comfortable, private space.

3. **Minimize Distractions**: Turn off notifications and give your partner your full attention during the check-in.

4. **Start Positively**: Begin each session by sharing something you're grateful for or a recent success.

5. **Balance Serious Discussion with Lightheartedness**: While the focus is on growth and accountability, allow room for humor and casual conversation to keep the atmosphere positive.

6. **End With Appreciation**: Conclude each session by expressing gratitude for your partner's support and insights.

7. **Follow Up**: Send a brief message after each check-in summarizing key points and expressing thanks.

Exercise: Designing Your Ideal Accountability Date

Objective: Plan the perfect setting and structure for your accountability check-ins.

Materials needed: Paper and pen or digital document, or do it down below.

Instructions:

1. Describe your ideal location or setup for your accountability meetings.

2. List any materials you want to have on hand (e.g., journal, goal tracker).

3. Outline a basic agenda for your "date," including:

   o opening ritual (e.g., sharing gratitude)

   o progress review

   o challenge discussion

187

o   goal setting

o   closing appreciation

_____

_____

_____

_____

4. Identify any potential obstacles to maintaining regular check-ins and brainstorm solutions.

_____

_____

_____

5. Set up the next three accountability dates in your calendar.

_____

_____

_____

_____

Reflection:

- How can you make these accountability check-ins something you look forward to?

- What boundaries might you need to set to ensure these meetings remain focused and productive?

Building Accountability Into Future Relationships

As you progress in your personal growth journey, it's important to integrate your newfound accountability practices into new relationships. This proactive approach can help prevent the recurrence of toxic patterns and foster healthier connections from the start.

How to Apply Accountability Tools to New Relationships

1. **Set Clear Expectations Early**: Communicate your commitment to personal growth and accountability from the beginning of new relationships.

2. **Share Your Growth Journey**: When appropriate, share insights from your accountability practices to model openness and self-reflection.

3. **Invite Feedback**: Create an atmosphere where open, honest feedback is welcomed and appreciated.

4. **Establish Check-In Rituals**: Introduce regular check-ins as a normal part of your relationship dynamics, whether with friends, romantic partners, or colleagues.

5. **Use "I" Statements**: Frame discussions about behavior and feelings using "I" statements to maintain responsibility for your own emotions and actions.

6. **Practice Active Listening**: Demonstrate your commitment to understanding others by using active listening techniques in your interactions.

7. **Acknowledge Mistakes Promptly**: When you slip into old patterns or make mistakes, acknowledge them quickly and take responsibility for making amends.

Exercise: Relationship Accountability Integration Plan
Objective: Create a plan for incorporating accountability practices into new relationships.

Materials needed: Paper and pen or digital document, or do it down below.

Instructions:

1. List 3-5 key accountability practices you want to maintain in new relationships.

2. For each practice, write a brief explanation of why it's important to you.

3. Draft a short script for introducing these practices to new friends, partners, or colleagues.

4. Identify potential challenges in implementing these practices in new relationships and brainstorm solutions.

Reflection:

- How might introducing these practices early in a relationship change its development?

- What concerns do you have about integrating accountability into new relationships, and how can you address them?

Recognizing Potential Toxic Behaviors Early in New Connections

Awareness of early warning signs can help you address potential issues before they become entrenched patterns. Here are some red flags to watch for:

- **Boundary Violations**: Pay attention to how new connections respect (or don't respect) your stated boundaries.

- **Emotional Manipulation**: Be wary of guilt-tripping, excessive flattery, or attempts to control your emotions.

- **Inconsistency**: Notice discrepancies between words and actions, or frequent mood swings that affect their behavior toward you.

- **Avoidance of Responsibility**: Observe how they handle mistakes or conflicts. Do they take responsibility or consistently blame others?

- **Lack of Reciprocity**: Ensure the relationship feels balanced in terms of emotional support, effort, and compromise.

- **Discomfort with Vulnerability**: Notice if there's resistance to open, honest communication about feelings and experiences.

- **Controlling Behavior**: Be alert to attempts to control your actions, relationships, or decisions.

Exercise: Personal Red Flag Inventory

Objective: Develop a personalized list of early warning signs based on past experiences and current boundaries.

Materials needed: Paper and pen or digital document, or do it down below.

Instructions:

1. Reflect on past relationships where toxic behaviors developed. What were the earliest signs that something was amiss?

2. List these early warning signs.

3. Add any additional red flags from the list above that resonate with you.

4. For each red flag, write a brief description of how it might manifest in a new relationship.

5. Develop a personal policy for how you'll address each red flag if you notice it in a new connection.

Reflection:

- How does having this inventory make you feel about entering new relationships?

- In what ways can you balance being alert to these warning signs with remaining open to new connections?

Maintaining Honesty and Openness in Future Interactions

Cultivating a practice of honesty and openness is crucial for building healthy, accountable relationships. Here are strategies to maintain this practice:

- **Commit to Radical Honesty**: Pledge to be truthful in all your interactions, even when it's uncomfortable.

- **Practice Vulnerability**: Share your thoughts, feelings, and experiences openly, modeling the depth of connection you seek.

195

- **Acknowledge Uncertainty**: It's okay to say, "I don't know," or "I'm not sure how I feel about that yet."

- **Express Needs Clearly**: Articulate your needs and expectations directly rather than hoping others will intuit them.

- **Offer Sincere Apologies**: When you make mistakes, apologize promptly and sincerely, focusing on how your actions impacted the other person.

- **Seek to Understand**: Approach disagreements with curiosity, seeking to understand the other person's perspective fully.

- **Regularly Check In**: Initiate conversations about the state of your relationship, discussing what's working well and what could be improved.

- **Be Open to Feedback**: Actively seek feedback from others and receive it graciously, even when it's difficult to hear.

- **Share Your Growth Journey**: Be open about your personal growth efforts, including your successes and struggles.

- **Practice Emotional Transparency**: Learn to articulate your emotions accurately and share them appropriately.

- **Avoid Assumptions**: Instead of assuming you know what others think or feel, ask for clarification.

- **Respect Privacy Boundaries**: While openness is important, also respect that everyone has the right to privacy. Be clear about your own boundaries and respect others'.

Exercise: Honesty and Openness Self-Assessment

Objective: Evaluate your current level of honesty and openness in relationships and identify areas for improvement.

Materials needed: Paper and pen or digital document, or do it down below.

Instructions:

1. Rate yourself on a scale of 1-10 (1 being lowest, 10 being highest) in the following areas:

   o   ability to express your true feelings

   o   comfort with vulnerability

   o   clarity in communicating needs and expectations

   o   openness to receiving feedback

   o   honesty about mistakes or shortcomings

   o   transparency about personal struggles

   o   ability to ask for help when needed

   o   comfort with initiating difficult conversations

2. For any areas where you rated yourself 7 or below, write a specific example of a recent situation where you struggled with honesty or openness.

3. For each situation, brainstorm how you could have approached it more honestly and openly.

4. Choose one area you'd like to focus on improving. Write down three specific actions you can take in the next week to practice greater honesty and openness in this area.

Reflection:

- What patterns do you notice in the areas where you struggle with honesty and openness?

- How might improving in your chosen area impact your relationships?

- What fears or concerns do you have about being more open and honest, and how can you address these?

Chapter Takeaways

Embracing Long-Term Accountability as a Lifestyle

As we conclude this section on sustaining long-term accountability, it's important to recognize that the practices and strategies we've explored are not just tools for overcoming toxic behaviors but foundations for a more fulfilling and authentic life. Long-term accountability is about more than just avoiding negative patterns; it's about continuously growing, deepening your relationships, and living in alignment with your values.

- **Consistency Is Key**: Regular check-ins, both with yourself and accountability partners, form the backbone of sustained change.

- **Tools Enhance Awareness**: Utilizing various assessment tools and journaling practices can significantly boost your self-awareness and ability to track progress.

- **Partnership Amplifies Growth**: Engaging in accountability partnerships provides support, perspective, and motivation that self-reflection alone cannot match.

- **Proactive Relationship Building**: Integrating accountability practices into new relationships from the start can prevent the development of toxic patterns.

- **Honesty and Openness are Practices**: Like any skill, maintaining honesty and openness in relationships requires consistent practice and refinement.

- **Flexibility is Vital**: As you grow and your circumstances change, be prepared to adjust your accountability practices to ensure they remain effective and relevant.

- **Self-Compassion Fuels Progress**: Remember to approach your accountability journey with kindness and understanding for yourself, recognizing that growth is a process with inevitable ups and downs.

Final Exercise: Your Accountability Manifesto

Objective: Create a personal manifesto that encapsulates your commitment to long-term accountability and growth.

Materials needed: Paper and pen or digital document, or do it down below.

Instructions:

1. Reflect on why accountability is important to you and how it aligns with your values and life goals.

2. Write a series of "I commit to..." statements that capture your dedication to accountability. For example:

   o "I commit to honest self-reflection on a weekly basis."

   o "I commit to seeking and graciously receiving feedback from others."

   o "I commit to taking responsibility for my actions and their impact on others."

3. Include specific practices you pledge to maintain based on what you've learned in this section.

4. Conclude with a statement about the kind of person you aim to become through this commitment to accountability.

5. Design or format your manifesto in a way that's visually appealing to you. Consider creating a version you can display where you'll see it regularly.

Reflection:

- How does creating this manifesto make you feel about your journey ahead?

- In what ways can you integrate this manifesto into your daily life to keep your commitment to accountability at the forefront of your mind?

As you move forward from this section, carry with you the understanding that sustaining long-term accountability is a dynamic, lifelong process. It requires courage, commitment, and compassion—for yourself and others. Remember that every step you take toward greater accountability is a step toward a more authentic, connected, and fulfilling life.

The journey of personal growth and overcoming toxic behaviors is rarely linear, but with the tools, strategies, and mindset you've developed here, you're well-equipped to navigate the challenges and celebrate the victories along the way. Trust in your capacity for change, lean on your support systems, and remain open to the transformative power of sustained accountability.

CONCLUSION

As we come to the end of this journey through understanding and overcoming toxic behaviors, it's essential to take a moment to reflect on how far we've come. The path we've traveled together has been challenging at times, requiring deep self-reflection, honesty, and a willingness to confront uncomfortable truths about ourselves and our relationships. But it has also been a journey of hope, growth, and the promise of healthier, more fulfilling connections with others and ourselves.

Recapping Our Journey

We began by exploring the roots of toxic behaviors, delving into the often painful experiences and unresolved traumas that can lead us to develop harmful patterns in our relationships. We learned that these behaviors, while destructive, are often misguided attempts to protect ourselves or meet unmet needs. This understanding has been crucial in developing compassion for ourselves and others, even as we work to change these patterns.

We then embarked on the challenging task of identifying our own toxic behaviors. Through various exercises and self-reflection prompts, we've learned to recognize the signs of manipulation, passive-aggression, and other harmful patterns in our own actions. This self-awareness, while sometimes uncomfortable, is the essential first step in making lasting change.

Our exploration of the impact of toxic behaviors on others has been particularly enlightening. By examining real-life stories and considering the perspective of those affected by our actions, we've deepened our empathy and understanding of the far-reaching consequences of our behavior. This awareness has served as a powerful motivator for change.

We've also looked inward, examining the toll that engaging in toxic behaviors takes on our own mental health. The guilt, anxiety, and depression that often accompany these patterns can create a vicious cycle, further reinforcing harmful behaviors. By understanding this connection, we've opened the door to breaking this cycle and fostering better mental health.

A significant portion of our journey has been dedicated to developing practical strategies for change. We've explored techniques for emotional regulation, effective communication, and boundary-setting. We've learned the importance of accountability and how to create support systems that foster growth and positive change.

Throughout this process, we've also touched on deeper psychological concepts, including aspects of dark psychology and narcissism. This knowledge has equipped us to recognize more insidious forms of manipulation and toxicity, both in ourselves and others, providing an additional layer of protection and understanding as we move forward.

The Transformative Power of Self-Awareness

One of the most profound lessons from this journey is the transformative power of self-awareness. By shining a light on our thoughts, emotions, and behaviors, we've taken the first crucial step toward change. Self-awareness allows us to:

- **Interrupt Automatic Responses**: We can now catch ourselves before reacting in old, harmful ways, creating a space for choice and more constructive responses.

- **Understand Our Triggers**: Recognizing what sets off our toxic behaviors enables us to either avoid these triggers or develop healthier coping mechanisms.

- **Connect With Our True Needs**: Often, toxic behaviors are misguided attempts to meet legitimate needs. Awareness helps us identify these needs and find healthier ways to fulfill them.

- **Cultivate Empathy**: Understanding our own pain and motivations fosters empathy for others, even when they're exhibiting toxic behaviors.

- **Track Our Progress**: Self-awareness allows us to notice and celebrate the positive changes we're making, no matter how small.

Remember, self-awareness is not about self-judgment or criticism. It's about observing ourselves with curiosity and compassion, always with the goal of growth and healing.

The Journey of Accountability

Another cornerstone of our work has been the concept of accountability. We've learned that taking responsibility for our actions, without excuses or deflection, is crucial for real change. Accountability involves:

- **Acknowledging the Impact**: Recognizing how our behaviors affect others, even when it's painful to do so.

- **Making Amends**: Taking concrete steps to repair the damage we've caused where possible.

- **Committing to Change**: Not just apologizing, but actively working to modify our behaviors.

- **Seeking Feedback**: Being open to hearing how our actions impact others and using this information to guide our growth.

- **Continuous Self-Reflection**: Regularly examining our behaviors and motivations to ensure we're staying on track.

Embracing accountability can be challenging, but it's also incredibly empowering. It puts us in the driver's seat of our own growth and healing.

The Role of Compassion in Healing

Throughout this book, we've emphasized the importance of self-compassion in the healing process. It's crucial to remember that toxic behaviors often stem from places of pain, insecurity, or unmet needs. While this doesn't excuse the behavior, understanding it can help us approach our healing journey with kindness and patience.

Compassion—both for ourselves and others—allows us to:

- **Face Difficult Truths**: When we approach our shortcomings with compassion, we're more able to confront and work on them.

- **Bounce Back from Setbacks**: Self-compassion helps us view slip-ups as learning opportunities rather than failures.

- **Extend Understanding to Others**: As we develop compassion for ourselves, we're better able to extend it to others, fostering healthier relationships.

- **Motivate Positive Change**: Contrary to what some might think, self-compassion doesn't lead to complacency. Instead, it provides a secure base from which we can take risks and make changes.

Remember, compassion doesn't mean excusing toxic behaviors. It means approaching the process of change with understanding and kindness, recognizing our shared human struggles and capacity for growth.

Building Healthy Relationships

As we've worked on overcoming toxic behaviors, we've also been laying the groundwork for healthier, more fulfilling relationships. The skills and insights we've gained equip us to:

- **Communicate Effectively**: We now have tools for expressing our needs and feelings clearly and respectfully.

- **Set and Respect Boundaries**: We understand the importance of personal boundaries and how to maintain them.

- **Handle Conflict Constructively**: Instead of resorting to manipulation or avoidance, we can approach conflicts as opportunities for understanding and growth.

- **Cultivate Emotional Intimacy**: By being more open and vulnerable, we can create deeper, more authentic connections.

- **Recognize Healthy Relationship Patterns**: We're better equipped to identify and foster relationships that are mutually supportive and growth-oriented.

Building healthy relationships is an ongoing process. It requires consistent effort, open communication, and a willingness to be vulnerable. But the rewards—deeper connections, mutual support, and shared growth—are immeasurable.

Ongoing Growth and Self-Care

As we conclude this book, it's important to remember that personal growth is a lifelong journey. The work we've done here is not a one-time fix but the beginning of an ongoing process of self-discovery and improvement. To support this continued growth:

- **Maintain Your Self-Reflection Practice**: Continue with regular check-ins, journaling, or whatever form of self-reflection works best for you.

- **Stay Connected With Your Support System**: Whether it's an accountability partner, a support group, or a therapist, maintain those connections that support your growth.

- **Keep Learning**: Stay curious about psychology, relationships, and personal development. There's always more to learn.

- **Practice Self-Care**: Remember to take care of your physical and emotional needs. Self-care is crucial for maintaining the energy and resilience needed for ongoing growth.

- **Celebrate Your Progress**: Take time to acknowledge how far you've come. Celebrating small victories reinforces positive change.

Dealing With Setbacks

Despite our best efforts, there will likely be times when we slip back into old patterns. When this happens:

1. **Don't Panic**: Setbacks are a normal part of the change process. They don't erase the progress you've made.

2. **Practice Self-Compassion**: Treat yourself with kindness. Remember, you're dealing with deeply ingrained patterns that take time to change.

3. **Reflect and Learn**: Use the setback as an opportunity to gain insight. What triggered the old behavior? What can you learn from this experience?

4. **Reach Out for Support**: Don't isolate yourself. Reach out to your support system for encouragement and perspective.

5. **Recommit to Your Goals**: Use the setback as motivation to recommit to your personal growth journey.

Remember, progress isn't linear. Setbacks don't define you; it's how you respond to them that matters.

The Ripple Effect of Personal Growth

As we work on ourselves and our relationships, it's important to recognize the broader impact of our efforts. By overcoming toxic behaviors and fostering healthier relationships, we create a ripple effect that extends far beyond our immediate circle. We:

- **Model Healthy Behavior**: Our growth can inspire and guide others on their own journeys.

- **Create Safer Spaces**: As we become more emotionally healthy, we contribute to creating environments where others feel safe to be vulnerable and authentic.

- **Break Generational Patterns**: By addressing our own toxic behaviors, we can help break cycles of harm that might otherwise be passed down to future generations.

- **Contribute to a More Compassionate World**: Every interaction where we choose empathy over judgment, understanding over reaction, contributes to a more compassionate society.

- **Enhance Our Communities**: Healthier individuals create healthier families, workplaces, and communities.

Your personal growth journey, while deeply personal, has the potential to create positive change far beyond yourself. This broader perspective can provide additional motivation and meaning to your efforts.

A New Chapter Begins

As we close this book, remember that this is not an ending but a beginning. You've gained valuable insights, tools, and strategies for overcoming toxic behaviors and building healthier relationships. Now, the real work of applying these lessons in your daily life begins.

There will be challenges ahead. Old patterns may resurface, and new obstacles may arise. But you now have a foundation of self-awareness, accountability, and compassion to guide you. You have strategies for self-reflection, tools for effective communication, and techniques for emotional regulation. Most importantly, you have a renewed commitment to your own growth and the well-being of your relationships.

Trust in your capacity for change. Believe in your worthiness of healthy, fulfilling relationships. Know that every small step you take toward growth and healing ripples out, positively affecting not just your life but the lives of those around you.

As you move forward from here, carry with you the knowledge that you are not alone on this journey. There are others walking similar paths and resources available if you need additional support. Stay connected with like-minded individuals who support your growth, and don't hesitate to seek professional help if you feel you need it.

Remember, the journey of personal growth is ongoing. There is no final destination, no point at which we can say we've "arrived." Instead, there is a continuous unfolding, a constant opportunity to learn, grow, and deepen our capacity for love, authenticity, and connection.

You've taken a courageous step by engaging with the material in this book. You've looked honestly at yourself, faced uncomfortable truths, and committed to positive change. That alone is worthy of celebration.

As you close this book and step back into your daily life, do so with pride in how far you've come, hope for the journey ahead, and compassion for yourself and others. You have within you the power to create meaningful change, nurture healthy relationships, and contribute to a more understanding and compassionate world.

The path ahead may not always be easy, but it is infinitely worthwhile. Embrace the journey, with all its challenges and rewards. Your future self—and all those whose lives you touch—will thank you for the important work you're doing.

Here's to your continued growth, healthier relationships, and the beautiful unfolding of your authentic self. The journey continues, and the best is yet to come.

THANK YOU FOR READING!

I hope *The How to Stop Being Toxic Workbook* provided you with valuable tools and insights for your journey toward healthier relationships and personal growth.

If you found this book helpful, a brief review on Amazon would mean so much. Your feedback not only supports my work but also helps others discover resources that might guide them on their own path to positive change.

To leave your review simply scan the QR code below:

And if you've already shared a review, thank you—I truly appreciate your support!

Wishing you all the best,

Caleb Petersen

Appendix A: More Practical Tools and Exercises

This appendix provides a collection of practical tools and exercises to support your journey in overcoming toxic behaviors and building healthier relationships. These resources are designed to be used in conjunction with the strategies and concepts discussed throughout the book.

Emotional Regulation Techniques

Emotional regulation is crucial in managing toxic behaviors. Here are several techniques to help you maintain emotional balance:

Box Breathing Exercise

Box breathing is a simple yet powerful technique for calming your nervous system:

1. Inhale slowly for a count of 4.

2. Hold your breath for a count of 4.

3. Exhale slowly for a count of 4.

4. Hold your breath for a count of 4.

5. Repeat for at least 4 cycles.

Practice this technique daily, and use it whenever you feel emotionally overwhelmed.

Progressive Muscle Relaxation Script

Find a comfortable position and follow this script:

1. Take a deep breath and close your eyes.

2. Focus on your feet. Tense all the muscles in your feet tightly. Hold for 5 seconds, then release. Notice the difference between tension and relaxation.

3. Move to your calves. Tense them tightly for 5 seconds, then release.

4. Continue this process, moving upward through your body: thighs, buttocks, abdomen, chest, hands, arms, shoulders, neck, and face.

5. After releasing the tension in your face, take a moment to notice how your entire body feels relaxed.

Self-Compassion Visualization

1. Close your eyes and take a few deep breaths.

2. Imagine yourself in a peaceful, comforting place.

3. Visualize a warm, gentle light surrounding you.

4. As you breathe in, imagine this light filling you with compassion and understanding.

5. As you breathe out, let go of any self-judgment or criticism.

6. Repeat to yourself: "I am worthy of compassion and understanding."

7. Continue for 5-10 minutes.

Grounding Technique: 5-4-3-2-1

Use this technique when you're feeling overwhelmed or anxious:

1. Identify 5 things you can see around you.

2. Identify 4 things you can touch or feel.

3. Identify 3 things you can hear.

4. Identify 2 things you can smell.

5. Identify 1 thing you can taste.

This exercise helps bring you back to the present moment, interrupting cycles of negative thoughts or emotions.

Communication Templates

Effective communication is key to overcoming toxic behaviors. Use these templates to guide your conversations:

"I" Statement Formula

Use this formula to express your feelings without blaming or attacking:

"I feel [emotion] when [specific situation] because [reason]. I need/would like [request]."

Examples:

- "I feel frustrated when plans are canceled at the last minute because it disrupts my schedule. If plans need to change, I would like to have at least a few hours' notice."

- "I feel hurt when my accomplishments aren't acknowledged because it makes me feel unappreciated. I need some recognition when I've worked hard on something."

Boundary Setting Script

Use this script to set clear, respectful boundaries:

1. Express appreciation: "I value our relationship and want to be honest with you."

2. State the issue: "When [specific behavior occurs], I feel [emotion]."

3. Make your request: "I would appreciate it if you could [desired behavior] instead."

4. Reaffirm the relationship: "I'm sharing this because I care about our relationship and want it to be healthy for both of us."

Example: "I value our friendship and want to be honest with you. I feel disrespected and frustrated when you show up late to our meetings without letting me know. I would appreciate it if you could text me if you're running late. I'm sharing this because I care about our friendship and want it to be healthy for both of us."

Sincere Apology Template

Follow this template to craft a meaningful apology:

1. Acknowledge the specific behavior: "I recognize that I [describe what you did]."

2. Take responsibility: "I understand that my actions [describe the impact]."

3. Express remorse: "I am truly sorry for [the behavior and its impact]."

4. Plan for change: "In the future, I will [describe how you'll behave differently]."

5. Ask for forgiveness: "I hope you can forgive me. Is there anything I can do to make this right?"

Example: "I recognize that I lashed out at you during our disagreement yesterday. I understand that my words were hurtful and made you feel disrespected. I am truly sorry for losing my temper and speaking to you that way. In the future, I will take a break to calm down before continuing difficult conversations. I hope you can forgive me. Is there anything I can do to make this right?"

Difficult Conversation Guide

Use this structure for navigating challenging discussions:

1. Opening: "I'd like to talk about [topic]. Is now a good time?"

2. State your intention: "My goal is to [your aim for the conversation]."

3. Describe the situation objectively: "I've noticed that [specific behavior or situation]."

4. Share your feelings and thoughts: "This makes me feel [emotion] because [reason]."

5. Listen actively to the other person's perspective.

6. Collaborate on a solution: "How can we work together to address this?"

7. Agree on next steps: "Let's recap what we've decided and follow up in [timeframe]."

Self-Reflection Questionnaires

Regular self-reflection is crucial for personal growth. Use these questionnaires to gain deeper insights:

Toxic Behavior Self-Assessment

Rate how often you engage in these behaviors (1 = never, 5 = very often):

1. I criticize others harshly or frequently.

2. I have difficulty admitting when I'm wrong.

3. I try to control others' behavior or decisions.

4. I give others the silent treatment when upset.

5. I make excuses for my hurtful behavior.

6. I struggle to respect others' boundaries.

7. I manipulate others to get what I want.

8. I have angry outbursts or temper tantrums.

9. I blame others for my problems or feelings.

10. I struggle to empathize with others' feelings.

Scoring: Add up your total.

- 10-20: Low toxicity

- 21-35: Moderate toxicity

- 36-50: High toxicity

Use this assessment to identify areas for improvement.

Relationship Patterns Questionnaire

For each of your close relationships, answer the following:

1. What recurring conflicts or issues arise in this relationship?

2. How do I typically react when these issues occur?

3. What unmet needs might be driving my behavior in this relationship?

4. What fears or insecurities come up for me in this relationship?

5. What positive patterns exist in this relationship?

6. How does this relationship compare to my ideal vision of a healthy relationship?

7. What steps can I take to improve this relationship?

Emotional Triggers Identification Worksheet

1. List 5 situations that consistently provoke strong negative emotions in you.

2. For each situation, describe:

o the emotion(s) you feel

o the intensity of the emotion (1-10)

o your typical reaction

o any past experiences this situation might be connected to

3. Reflect on patterns:

o Are there common themes among your triggers?

o How do your reactions impact your relationships?

o What healthier responses could you practice in these situations?

Personal Values Clarification Exercise

1. From the following list, circle the 10 values that resonate most with you:

o honesty

o compassion

- success

- family

- independence

- creativity

- loyalty

- adventure

- knowledge

- spirituality

- health

- friendship

- justice

- authenticity

- security

- growth

- harmony

- respect

- fun

- contribution

2. Narrow your list to the top 5 values.

3. For each of these 5 values, write:

   o why this value is important to you

   o how you currently honor this value in your life

   o how you could better align your behavior with this value

4. Reflect on how these values can guide your behavior in challenging situations.

Goal-Setting and Progress-Tracking Tools

Setting clear goals and tracking your progress is essential for lasting change.

SMART Goals Worksheet for Behavior Change

Use this framework to set effective goals:

- Specific: What exactly do you want to achieve?

- Measurable: How will you know when you've achieved it?

- Achievable: Is this goal realistic given your current circumstances?

- Relevant: How does this goal align with your values and long-term objectives?

- Time-bound: By when do you want to achieve this goal?

Example:

- S: I want to reduce my angry outbursts at work.

- M: I will have no more than one outburst per week.

- A: This is achievable with practice in emotional regulation techniques.

- R: This aligns with my value of professionalism and desire for better work relationships.

- T: I will achieve this within two months.

Create 2-3 SMART goals for yourself related to overcoming toxic behaviors.

Weekly Progress Tracking Template

Use this template to monitor your progress:

Week of: [Date]

1. This week's focus goal:

2. Actions taken toward goal:

3. Successes this week:

4. Challenges faced:

5. Lessons learned:

6. Next week's plan:

Rate your overall progress this week (1-10):

Setback Analysis Form

When you experience a setback, use this form to learn from it:

1. Describe the setback: What happened?

2. Identify triggers: What led to this setback?

3. Emotional state: How were you feeling before and during the setback?

4. Thought patterns: What thoughts were going through your mind?

5. Behavior: How did you react?

6. Consequences: What was the outcome of your behavior?

7. Alternative responses: How could you have handled this differently?

8. Learning: What can you learn from this experience?

9. Prevention: How can you prevent similar setbacks in the future?

Long-Term Vision Board Exercise

Creating a vision board can help you stay motivated and focused on your long-term goals.

Materials needed:

- large paper or corkboard

- magazines

- scissors

- glue or pins

Instructions:

1. Reflect on your ideal future self, free from toxic behaviors. How do you behave? How do your relationships look?

2. Browse through magazines and cut out images, words, or phrases that represent this vision.

3. Arrange these elements on your board in a way that's meaningful to you.

4. Add personal touches: Write affirmations or goals directly on the board.

5. Place your vision board where you'll see it daily.

6. Spend a few minutes each day visualizing yourself living this reality.

7. Update your board periodically as your goals and vision evolve.

Remember, change is a journey, not a destination. Use these tools regularly to support your ongoing growth and development. Be patient with yourself, celebrate your progress, and don't hesitate to seek additional support when needed. Your commitment to overcoming toxic behaviors and building healthier relationships is commendable, and with consistent effort and self-reflection, you can create lasting positive change in your life and relationships.

Appendix B: Additional Resources and Further Reading

This appendix provides a comprehensive list of resources to support your ongoing journey in overcoming toxic behaviors and building healthier relationships. From books and online resources to therapy guides and crisis support, these materials are designed to complement the strategies and concepts discussed throughout the book.

Recommended Reading List

The following books offer deeper insights into toxic behaviors, personal growth, and relationship dynamics. They are categorized for easy reference:

Understanding Toxic Behaviors and Their Roots

- *Toxic Parents: Overcoming Their Hurtful Legacy and Reclaiming Your Life* by Susan Forward

o A groundbreaking book that explores how childhood experiences shape adult behaviors.

- *Why Does He Do That? Inside the Minds of Angry and Controlling Men* by Lundy Bancroft

o Offers insights into abusive behaviors, particularly useful for those dealing with toxic relationships.

- *Adult Children of Emotionally Immature Parents* by Lindsay C. Gibson

o Explores how childhood emotional neglect impacts adult behavior and relationships.

- *Emotional Blackmail* by Susan Forward

o Examines manipulative behaviors and offers strategies for breaking free from emotional manipulation.

Self-Help and Personal Growth

- *Nonviolent Communication: A Language of Life* by Marshall B. Rosenberg

o Introduces a communication framework that promotes empathy and understanding.

- *The Gifts of Imperfection* by Brené Brown

o Explores the power of vulnerability and authenticity in overcoming shame and fostering self-acceptance.

- *Mindset: The New Psychology of Success* by Carol S. Dweck

o Discusses how our mindset shapes our behavior and ability to grow and change.

- *The Body Keeps the Score* by Bessel van der Kolk

o Examines the effects of trauma on the body and mind, offering insights into healing.

Improving Relationships

- *Attached: The New Science of Adult Attachment and How It Can Help You Find—and Keep—Love* by Amir Levine and Rachel Heller

o Explores attachment theory and its impact on adult relationships.

- *The Seven Principles for Making Marriage Work* by John Gottman

o While focused on marriage, offers valuable insights for all types of relationships.

- *Crucial Conversations: Tools for Talking When Stakes Are High* by Kerry Patterson et al.

o Provides strategies for navigating difficult conversations in all areas of life.

- *The 5 Love Languages* by Gary Chapman

o Explores different ways people give and receive love, promoting understanding in relationships.

Memoirs and Personal Accounts

- *Educated* by Tara Westover

o A memoir that illustrates the journey of overcoming a toxic family environment.

- *The Glass Castle* by Jeannette Walls

o A powerful memoir about resilience and breaking cycles of dysfunction.

- *Know My Name* by Chanel Miller

o A memoir that addresses trauma, healing, and reclaiming one's narrative.

Academic and Professional Texts

- *The Oxford Handbook of Personality Disorders* edited by Thomas A. Widiger

o A comprehensive academic resource on personality disorders, including those associated with toxic behaviors.

- *Cognitive Behavioral Therapy: Basics and Beyond* by Judith S. Beck

o An in-depth look at CBT techniques, useful for understanding therapeutic approaches to behavior change.

- *The Handbook of Conflict Resolution: Theory and Practice* by Peter T. Coleman et al.

- o A comprehensive resource on understanding and resolving conflicts in various contexts.

Online Resources

The internet offers a wealth of information and support. Here are some reputable online resources:

Websites for Mental Health Information

- National Institute of Mental Health (www.nimh.nih.gov)
- o Offers evidence-based information on mental health conditions and treatments.
- Psychology Today (www.psychologytoday.com)
- o Provides articles on various mental health topics and a therapist directory.
- MentalHealth.gov (www.mentalhealth.gov)
- o Offers resources and information on mental health in the United States.
- Mind (www.mind.org.uk)
- o A UK-based charity providing information and support for mental health issues.
- Online Support Groups and Forums
- 7 Cups (www.7cups.com)
- ■ Offers online therapy and free support chat rooms.
- o NAMI Connection Support Group (www.nami.org/Support-Education/Support-Groups)
- ■ Peer-led support groups for adults living with mental health conditions.
- o Reddit Communities

- r/DecidingToBeBetter

- r/selfimprovement

- r/getting_over_it (Note: While these can be supportive communities, always approach online forums with caution and prioritize your privacy and safety.)

Recommended Apps

- Headspace: For meditation and mindfulness practice

- Daylio: For mood tracking and journaling

- Calm Harm: For managing self-harm urges

- Sanvello: For stress, anxiety, and depression management

- Gottman Card Decks: For improving relationship communication

Podcasts on Personal Growth and Relationships

- "Where Should We Begin?" with Esther Perel

o Real couples anonymously share their stories in one-time therapy sessions.

- "The Happiness Lab" with Dr. Laurie Santos

o Explores scientific research on happiness and well-being.

- "Unlocking Us" with Brené Brown

o Conversations about emotions, relationships, and the human experience.

- "The Psychology Podcast" with Scott Barry Kaufman

o Explores human behavior and the mind.

- "Therapist Uncensored" with Sue Marriott and Ann Kelley

o Discusses attachment, relationships, and personal growth.

Therapy and Professional Support Guide

Seeking professional help can be a crucial step in overcoming toxic behaviors. Here's a guide to help you navigate this process:

Types of Therapy Beneficial for Overcoming Toxic Behaviors

- **Cognitive Behavioral Therapy (CBT)**

o Focuses on identifying and changing negative thought patterns and behaviors.

- **Dialectical Behavior Therapy (DBT)**

o Teaches skills for emotional regulation, distress tolerance, and interpersonal effectiveness.

- **Psychodynamic Therapy**

o Explores how past experiences influence current behaviors and relationships.

- **Eye Movement Desensitization and Reprocessing (EMDR)**

o Particularly useful for processing traumatic experiences that may contribute to toxic behaviors.

- **Schema Therapy**

o Addresses early maladaptive schemas that contribute to negative patterns in life.

- **Group Therapy**

o Provides peer support and opportunities to practice new behaviors in a safe environment.

How to Choose a Therapist

1. Determine what type of professional you need (psychiatrist, psychologist, counselor, etc.).

2. Check their credentials and specializations.

3. Consider their therapeutic approach and ensure it aligns with your needs.

4. Verify that they're licensed in your state or country.

5. Check if they accept your insurance or offer sliding scale fees.

6. Schedule an initial consultation to assess your comfort level with them.

Questions to Ask a Potential Therapist

- What experience do you have treating individuals with toxic behavior patterns?

- What is your approach to therapy?

- How do you typically structure sessions?

- How do you measure progress in therapy?

- What role do you see me playing in my own healing process?

- How long do you typically work with clients addressing similar issues?

What to Expect in Therapy

1. **Initial Assessment**: Your therapist will gather information about your history and current concerns.

2. **Goal Setting**: You'll work together to establish clear objectives for therapy.

3. **Regular Sessions**: Typically weekly, these involve discussions, exercises, and skill-building.

4. **Homework**: Many therapists assign tasks to complete between sessions.

5. **Progress Review**: Periodically, you'll assess your progress and adjust goals as needed.

6. **Termination**: As you achieve your goals, you'll work with your therapist to plan for ending therapy.

Alternative Support Options

- **Life Coaches**: Can help with goal-setting and personal development but are not mental health professionals.

- **Support Groups**: Offer peer support for specific issues (e.g., Al-Anon for families affected by alcoholism).

- **Spiritual Counselors**: For those seeking support within their faith tradition.

- **Employee Assistance Programs (EAPs)**: Many workplaces offer free, short-term counseling services.

Crisis Resources

In times of crisis, it's crucial to have immediate support available. Here are some resources:

Hotlines

- National Suicide Prevention Lifeline (USA): 1-800-273-8255

o Available 24-7 for anyone in suicidal crisis or emotional distress.

- Crisis Text Line: Text HOME to 741741 (USA)

o 24-7 support via text message.

- National Domestic Violence Hotline (USA): 1-800-799-7233

o Offers support for those experiencing domestic violence.

- SAMHSA National Helpline (USA): 1-800-662-4357

o For individuals facing mental health or substance use disorders.

- The Trevor Project (USA): 1-866-488-7386

o Crisis intervention for LGBTQ+ youth.

International Resources

- Befrienders Worldwide (befrienders.org)

o Provides links to helplines in countries around the world.

- International Association for Suicide Prevention (iasp.info)

o Offers a directory of crisis centers globally.

Creating a Personal Crisis Plan

1. Identify your personal warning signs of a developing crisis.

2. List coping strategies that have worked for you in the past.

3. Write down contact information for your support network.

4. Include contact details for your therapist or local crisis services.

5. List any current medications and dosages.

6. Identify a safe place you can go if you need to leave your current environment.

7. Write an encouraging message to yourself to read during difficult moments.

Keep this plan easily accessible, and share it with trusted individuals in your support network.

Glossary of Key Terms

Understanding the terminology used in discussing toxic behaviors and mental health can be empowering. Here's a brief glossary of key terms:

- **Gaslighting**: A form of manipulation that causes someone to question their own perceptions and reality.

- **Trauma Bonding**: A psychological response to abuse where the victim forms a strong emotional attachment to their abuser.

- **Cognitive Distortions**: Inaccurate thoughts that reinforce negative thinking patterns.

- **Boundaries**: Limits we set with others to protect our physical and emotional well-being.

- **Emotional Dysregulation**: Difficulty in managing emotional responses.

- **Narcissistic Personality Disorder**: A mental condition characterized by an inflated sense of self-importance and a deep need for excessive attention and admiration.

- **Codependency**: A dysfunctional relationship dynamic where one person supports or enables another's addiction, poor mental health, or immaturity.

- **Resilience**: The ability to recover from or adjust easily to misfortune or change.

- **Mindfulness**: The practice of maintaining a nonjudgmental state of heightened or complete awareness of one's thoughts, emotions, or experiences on a moment-to-moment basis.

- **Projection**: A defense mechanism where a person attributes their own unacceptable thoughts or feelings to someone else.

Remember, this glossary is not exhaustive, and these terms should not be used for self-diagnosis. Always consult with a mental health professional for proper diagnosis and treatment.

As you continue your journey of growth and healing, these resources can provide additional support and information. Remember that overcoming toxic behaviors is a process, and it's okay to seek help along the way. Your commitment to personal growth and building healthier relationships is commendable. Keep moving forward, one step at a time.

References

American Psychological Association. (2020). Publication manual of the American Psychological Association (7th ed.). https://doi.org/10.1037/0000165-000

Anonymous. (n.d.). [Quote about thoughts becoming destiny].

Bancroft, L. (2002). Why does he do that?: Inside the minds of angry and controlling men. Berkley Books.

Beck, J. S. (2011). Cognitive behavior therapy: Basics and beyond (2nd ed.). Guilford Press.

Brown, B. (2010). The gifts of imperfection: Let go of who you think you're supposed to be and embrace who you are. Hazelden Publishing.

Chapman, G. (2015). The 5 love languages: The secret to love that lasts. Northfield Publishing.

Coleman, P. T., Deutsch, M., & Marcus, E. C. (Eds.). (2014). The handbook of conflict resolution: Theory and practice (3rd ed.). Jossey-Bass.

Dweck, C. S. (2006). Mindset: The new psychology of success. Random House.

Forward, S. (1989). Toxic parents: Overcoming their hurtful legacy and reclaiming your life. Bantam Books.

Forward, S., & Frazier, D. (1997). Emotional blackmail: When the people in your life use fear, obligation, and guilt to manipulate you. HarperCollins Publishers.

Fromm, E. (1956). The Art of Loving. Harper & Brothers.

Gibson, L. C. (2015). Adult children of emotionally immature parents: How to heal from distant, rejecting, or self-involved parents. New Harbinger Publications.

Gottman, J. M., & Silver, N. (2015). The seven principles for making marriage work: A practical guide from the country's foremost relationship expert. Harmony Books.

Jung, C. G. (1989). Memories, dreams, reflections (A. Jaffé, Ed.; R. Winston & C. Winston, Trans.). Vintage Books. (Original work published 1963)

Levine, A., & Heller, R. (2010). Attached: The new science of adult attachment and how it can help you find - and keep - love. Penguin Books.

Miller, C. (2019). Know my name: A memoir. Viking.

National Institute of Mental Health. (2021). Mental health information. https://www.nimh.nih.gov/health/topics

Patterson, K., Grenny, J., McMillan, R., & Switzler, A. (2012). Crucial conversations: Tools for talking when stakes are high (2nd ed.). McGraw-Hill Education.

Perel, E. (Host). (2017-present). Where should we begin? [Audio podcast]. Audible Originals. https://www.estherperel.com/podcast

Rosenberg, M. B. (2015). Nonviolent communication: A language of life (3rd ed.). PuddleDancer Press.

Santos, L. (Host). (2019-present). The happiness lab [Audio podcast]. Pushkin Industries. https://www.happinesslab.fm/

Substance Abuse and Mental Health Services Administration. (2021). National helpline. https://www.samhsa.gov/find-help/national-helpline

The Trevor Project. (2021). For young LGBTQ lives. https://www.thetrevorproject.org/

van der Kolk, B. (2014). The body keeps the score: Brain, mind, and body in the healing of trauma. Viking.

Walls, J. (2005). The glass castle: A memoir. Scribner.

Westover, T. (2018). Educated: A memoir. Random House.

Wetzler, S. (1992). Living with the passive-aggressive man: Coping with hidden aggression - from the bedroom to the boardroom. Fireside.

Widiger, T. A. (Ed.). (2012). The Oxford handbook of personality disorders. Oxford University Press.